PLANNING

USING

PRIMAVERA

SURETRAK® PROJECT MANAGER

VERSION 3.0

PAUL EASTWOOD HARRIS

DISCLAIMER
The information contained in this workbook is to the best of the author's knowledge true and correct. The author has made every effort to ensure accuracy but cannot be held responsible for any loss or damage arising from any information in this book.

AUTHOR AND PUBLISHER	**DISTRIBUTED BY**
Paul E Harris	Writersandpoets USA
Eastwood Harris Pty Ltd	2901 W. Queen Lane C
PO Box 4032	Philadelphia, PA 19129
Doncaster Heights 3109	United States
Victoria, Australia	

Email:	harrispe@eh.com.au	Email:	Sales@bestpmbooks.com
Web:	http://www.eh.com.au	Web:	http://www.bestpmbooks.com
Tel:	+61 (0)4 1118 7701	Toll Free:	1800 452 5205 Ext 00
Fax:	+61 (0)3 9846 7700	Tel:	+1 215 438 5641
		Fax:	+1 215 438 5961

Please send any comments on this publication to the author.

ACKNOWLEDGEMENTS

The author would like to acknowledge D. Grant for his initial assistance supplying material which forms the basis of some chapters in this publication.

US English Version, 26 October 2002.

ISBN: 0 9577783 2 5

1   INTRODUCTION

1.1   Purpose

The purpose of this book is to provide you with a method for planning and controlling projects using Primavera SureTrak Project Manager Version 3.0. At the end of the book you should be able to:

- Understand the steps required to create a project plan

- Set up the SureTrak software

- Define calendars

- Define activity codes

- Add and organize activities

- Add the logic

- Format the display

- Filter and store layouts

- Print reports

- Record and track progress

- Customize the project options

- Create and assign resources

- Understand the impact of activity types and driving resources

- Understand the different techniques for scheduling

- Use the different project utilities

The book does not cover every aspect of SureTrak, but it does cover all the main features required for scheduling. It provides a solid grounding, which enables you to learn the other features of the software from the help, files and manuals.

There are workshops at the end of each chapter and completed workshops in SureTrak format may be downloaded from the Eastwood Harris web site at http://www.eh.com.au.

1.2 *Required Background Knowledge*

This book does not intend to teach you how to use computers or to project manage. The book is intended to teach you how to use SureTrak in a project environment. Therefore, to be able to follow this book you should have the following background knowledge:

- The ability to use a personal computer and understand the fundamentals of the operating system;

- Have used application software such as Microsoft Office software which would have given you exposure to Windows menu systems and typical Windows functions such as copy and paste;

- An understanding of how projects are managed, such as the phases and processes that take place over the lifetime of a project.

1.3 *Purpose of Planning*

The ultimate purpose of planning is to build a model that allows you to predict which activities and resources are critical to the timely completion of the project. Strategies may then be implemented to ensure that these activities and resources are managed, ensuring the project is delivered both **On Time** and **Within Budget**.

Planning helps to avoid:

- Loss of revenue

- Loss of a facility

- Additional changeover costs

- Inconvenience costs

- Contractual disputes

- Extensions of time claims

Planning aims to:

- Optimize time

- Evaluate different methods

- Optimize resources

- Provide early warning of potential problems

- Enable you to take proactive and not reactive action

1.4 Project Planning Metrics

The three components that you may measure and control using a planning and scheduling software are time, cost and effort (resources).

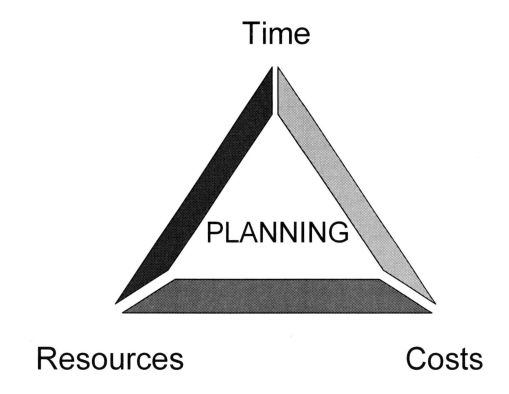

Any change in one normally results in a change in one or both of the other two.

1.5 Planning Cycle

The planning cycle is an integral part of managing a project. A software package such as SureTrak makes this task much easier.

When the original plan is agreed the **Baseline** is set. The **Baseline** is a record of the original plan. The **Baseline** dates may be recorded in SureTrak in data fields titled **Target Start** and **Target Finish**

The actual progress is monitored and recorded during project execution and compared to the **Target dates**.

The progress is reported and evaluated. The plan may be changed by adding or deleting activities and adjusting Remaining Durations or Resources. A revised plan is then published.

2   CREATING A PROJECT PLAN

The aim of this chapter is to give you an understanding of what a plan is and some practical guidance on how your schedule may be created and statused as part of a project.

2.1   *Understanding Planning and Scheduling Software*

The project is essentially a set of operations or activities to be completed in logical order. A schedule is an attempt to model these operations and their relationships. These operations take time to accomplish and may employ resources that have limited availability.

Planning and scheduling software allows the user to:

- Break a project down into activities that are entered into the software;

- Nominate durations, predecessors and successors of the activities and then calculate the start and finish date of all the activities;

- Assign resources, which represent people, equipment or materials, to the activities and calculate the project resource requirements;

- Monitor the actual progress of activities against the original plan and amend the plan when required;

- Monitor the consumption of resources and re-estimate the resources required to finish the project;

There are four modes or levels in which planning and scheduling software may be used.

	Planning	**Tracking**
Without Resources	**LEVEL 1** Planning without Resources	**LEVEL 2** Tracking progress without Resources
With Resources	**LEVEL 3** Planning with Resources	**LEVEL 4** Tracking progress with Resources

As the level increases, the amount of information required to maintain the schedule will increase, and more importantly, your skill and knowledge in using the software will also have to increase. This book is designed to take you from Level 1 to Level 4.

2.2 Understanding your Project

Before you start the process of creating a project plan, it is important to have an understanding of the project and how it is planned to be executed. On large complex projects, this information is usually available from the following types of documents:

- Project scope

- Functional specification

- Requirements baseline

- Contract documentation

- Plans and drawings

- Project execution plan

- Contracting and purchasing plan

- Equipment lists

- Installation plan

- Testing plan

It is important to gain a good understanding of the project process before starting to plan your project. You should also understand what level of reporting is required, as providing too little or too much detail will often lead to the schedule being discarded.

There are three processes required to create or maintain a plan at each level:

- Collecting the relevant project data;

- Entering and manipulating the data in software;

- Distributing the plan, reviewing and revising.

The ability to collect the data is as important as the ability to enter and manipulate the information into the software. On larger projects it may be necessary to write policies and procedures to ensure accurate collection of data from the various departments and sites.

2.3 Level 1 – Planning Without Resources

This is the simplest mode of planning.

2.3.1 Creating Projects

To create the project you will require the following information:

- Project Name

- Client Name

- Other information such as Location

- The Start Date (and perhaps the Finish Date)

2.3.2 Defining Calendars

Before you start entering activities into your schedule it is advisable to set up the calendars. These are used to model the working time for each activity in the project. For example, a six-day calendar is created for those activities that will be worked for six days a week. The calendars should include any public holidays and any other exceptions to available working days such as Rostered Days Off (RDO).

2.3.3 Defining Activity Codes

Activity Codes are used to sort, select, summarize and group activities. Before creating a dictionary of valid Activity Codes ask the following questions:

- How many phases are there? (E.g. Design, Procure, Install and Test)

- How many disciplines are there? (E.g. Civil, Mechanical and Electrical)

- Which departments are involved in the project? (E.g. Sales, Procurement and Installation)

- What work is expected to be contracted out?

- How many sites or areas are there in the project?

Use the responses to these questions to create the Activity Code dictionaries.

2.3.4 Adding and Organizing Activities

Activities must be defined before they are entered into the schedule. It is important that you carefully consider:

- The scope of the activity.

- How long the task is going to take?

- Who is going to do it?

- What the deliverable is for each activity?

The project estimate is usually a good place to start looking for a breakdown of the project into tasks, resources and costs. It may even give an indication of how long the work will take.

Usually project reports are created on a regular basis, such as every week or every month. "Good Practice" says that an activity should not span more than two reporting periods. That way the activities should only be "In Progress" for one period. If an activity is "In-Progress" for more than two periods then it has slipped.

It is also good practice to have a measurable finish point for each group of activities. The issue of documentation to mark the end of one task and the start point of another adds to the clarity of a schedule. Examples of document issues are:

- Issue of a Drawing Package
- Completion of a Specification
- Placing of an Order
- Delivery Dockets
- Testing Certificates for Equipment

The activities are then added to the schedule and assigned their Activity Codes so that they may be sorted and grouped.

2.3.5 Adding the Logic Links
The logic is then added to provide the order in which the activities must be undertaken and the schedule will calculate the start and finish dates for each activity.

It is good practice to create a **Closed Network** with the logic. In a **Closed Network** all activities have one or more predecessors and one or more successors except:

- The project start milestone or first activity that has no predecessors, and
- The finish milestone or finish activity that has no successors.

Thus when the logic is correctly applied, a delay to an activity will delay all successor activities and the project end date when there is insufficient spare time or **Float** to accommodate the delay.

To correctly model the impact of events outside the logical sequence you may use constraints to nominate specific dates such as the availability of a facility. Constraints should be cross-referenced to the supporting documentation.

2.3.6 Scheduling the Project
The software will calculate the shortest time in which the project may be completed.

It will also identify the **Critical Path(s)**. The Critical Path is the chain(s) of activities that takes the longest time to accomplish. This will define the Earliest Finish date of the project. The calculated completion date depends on the critical activities starting and finishing on time – if they are delayed, the whole project will be delayed.

Activities that may be delayed without affecting the project end date have **Float**.

Total Float is the amount of time an activity may be delayed without delaying the project end date. The delay of an activity with Total Float may delay other activities with Total Float.

Free Float is the amount of time an activity may be delayed without delaying the start date of another activity.

2.3.7   Formatting the Display – Filters and Layouts

There are tools to manipulate and display the activities to suit the project reporting requirements.

2.3.8   Printing and Reports

There are facilities that allow you to present the information in a clear and concise manner to communicate the requirements to all project members.

2.3.9   Issuing the Plan

All members of the project team should review the project plan in an attempt to optimize the process and methods employed.

Reports should be used to communicate what is expected of team members while providing each with the opportunity to further improve the outcome.

2.4   Level 2 – Monitoring Progress Without Resources

2.4.1   Setting the Target Schedule

The optimized and agreed plan is used as a baseline for future comparisons. The software can record the baseline dates for comparison against actual progress during the life of the project. These planned dates are stored in the **Target date** fields.

2.4.2   Tracking Progress

The schedule should be **Statused** (updated or progressed) on a regular basis and progress is recorded at that point in time. The date on which progress is reported is known as the **Data Date**. Whatever the frequency chosen for statusing, you will have to collect the following activity information in order to status a schedule:

- Actual Start Dates of started activities

- Percentage Completed

- Remaining Duration for started, but incomplete activities

- Actual Finish Dates for completed activities

- Any revisions to activities that have not started

The schedule may be statused after this information has been collected, and then the recorded progress compared to the **Target** dates.

At this point in time it may be necessary to further optimize the schedule.

2.5 Level 3 – Scheduling With Resources

2.5.1 Creating and Using Resources

Firstly, a resource pool is established by entering the project resources into the software. You then assign the required quantity of each resource to the activities.

Entering a cost rate for each resource enables you to conduct cost analysis such as comparing the cost of supplementing overloading resources against the cost of extending the project deadline.

Time-phased cash flows and budgets may be automatically produced from this resource/cost data.

2.5.2 Activity Types and Driving Resources

These are additional features that enable the user to more accurately model real life situations.

2.6   Level 4 – Monitoring Progress of a Resourced Schedule

2.6.1   Statusing Projects with Resources

When you status a project with resources you will need to collect some additional information:

- The quantities or costs spent to date per activity for each resource, and

- The quantities or costs required per resource to complete each activity.

You may then status a resourced schedule with this data.

2.7   Additional Features

2.7.1   Tools and Techniques for Scheduling

At this point the book covers some additional scheduling techniques.

2.7.2   Project Utilities

Project Utilities are administration tools that are covered last.

3   CREATING PROJECTS AND SETTING UP THE SOFTWARE

There are three methods of creating a new project in SureTrak:

- Use a template that contains default data and formats

- Copy an old project and modify it

- Use the SureTrak Project KickStart Wizard

Before creating a project file you must understand the file types SureTrak will work with.

3.1   File Types

SureTrak will work with four file types:

- **SureTrak** is the standard format for SureTrak files and allows **Long File Names** (SureTrak Version 2.0 allowed a maximum of eight characters in the file name).

- **Project Groups** is used when you have a number of projects sharing the same resources and must have exactly four characters in the file name.

- **Concentric (P3)** is used when you wish to share the project with P3 users and must have exactly four characters in the file name.

- **MPX** is a Microsoft Project text data format that many planning and scheduling software packages use to interchange data. MPP is the native Microsoft Project file format, which may not be read by SureTrak.

All file types except MPX will create a number of files in the selected directory for each project with the Project Name as part of the file name.

Notes for Concentric (P3) users

- When using **Concentric (P3)** format the Target dates are set in P3 and can not be changed with SureTrak.

- The Targets dates may viewed but not be set with SureTrak.

- The Target dates viewed in SureTrak are read from the Target 1 project set at Project level not at Project Group level. Therefore, a Target 1 must be set for each Project in P3 when Project Groups are being used.

- Users may open the same file in **Project Group** format or **Concentric (P3)** format, the difference being how the Target dates are treated. In **Project Group** format the Target dates may be set in SureTrak.

3.2 Creating a New Project from a Template

After starting SureTrak select **File**, **New** to create a new project from a template. The title page contains important set-up information for the calendars as well as setting defaults such as file location, type and version. This data may be edited in the **Project Overview** form found under **File**, **Project Overview**.

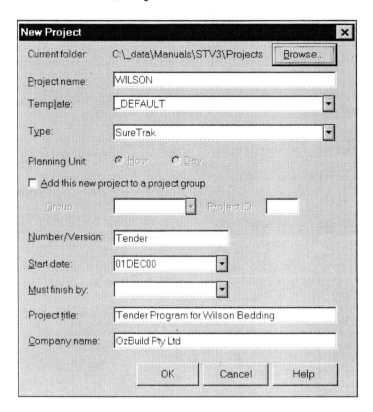

- Use **Current Folder** and to select where your project files are stored.
- The **Project Name** may:
  - ➤ Use long file names when **Type** is **SureTrak**
  - ➤ Must be exactly four characters when **Type** is **Concentric (P3)** or **Project Groups**.

- Select a Project **Template**. Templates hold default Calendars, Resources, Activity Codes, Activities, Relationships and Resources Assignments.

- **Planning Unit** of days or hours is selected when the Project Type is Concentric (P3) or Project Groups.

- **Add this new project to a project group** allows you to create a project as a member of a **Project Group**, like a subproject. Select the **Project Group** as the Project Type and nominate a two Character ID that must start with a letter. This new project will share data such as calendars, resources and codes with all other projects in the Project Group.

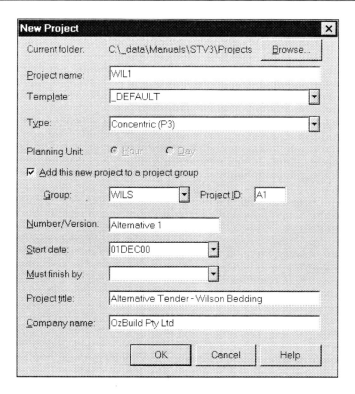

To save time when you create new projects, you should create your own templates to suit the different types of projects your organization undertakes. Create a template by saving a project with or without activities in the template subdirectory.

- **Number/Version** is a description that is visible when using **File, Open**.

- **Start date**, SureTrak will not schedule activities before this date.

- **Must finish by** is an optional field. This imposes a late finish date on the project. Total float is calculated to this date if it is completed.

- **Project title** is shown in the **File, Open** form and may be referenced in printed reports.

- **Company name** may be referenced in printed reports only.

WORKSHOP 1

Creating our Project

Preamble

OzBuild has been short listed by Wilson Bedding for a project and will be bidding. You have been advised that the RFP (Request For Price) will not be available until 1st December 2003.

You are an employee of OzBuild Pty Ltd and are responsible for planning the bid preparation required to ensure that a response to an RFP from Wilson Bedding is submitted on time.

Assignment

1. Create the project using the information below.

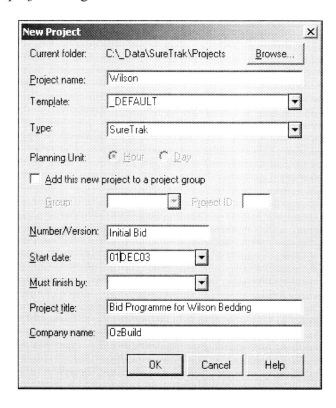

2. Save your project.

Note: Completed workshops in SureTrak format may be downloaded from the Eastwood Harris web site at http://www.eh.com.au.

3.3 Opening an Existing Project

The second method of creating a new schedule is to open an existing schedule and modifying it. Select **File**, **Open** or **Ctrl O** to display the **Open Project** form below.

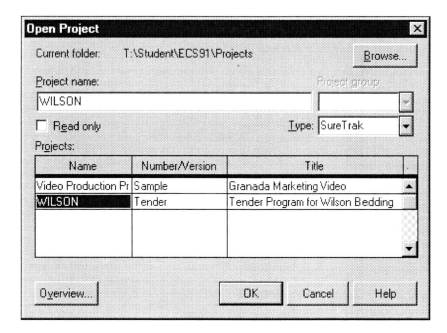

- Use ⌈Browse...⌉ to select the **Current Folder** where the existing project is located.

- Select the file type from the **Type** drop-down box.

- Check the **Read only** box if you do not want to edit any information in the project.

- Select the existing project you wish to open.

- Click **OK** to open the project.

- Click on ⌈Overview...⌉ to open the **Project Overview** to display additional project information.

Then use **File**, **Save As** or **F12** to save the file under a different name.

- Enter a new Project Name.

- Select which **Current Folder** you which to save the project.

- Select the file type from the drop-down box.

- Click on **OK** to save the new project.

You may now alter the contents of this existing plan to reflect the scope of your new project.

SureTrak allows you to have up to four projects open at any one time.

3.4   Using the SureTrak KickStart Wizard

The third method of creating a new project is to use **Tools**, **Wizards**, **Project Kickstart Wizard** or selecting the 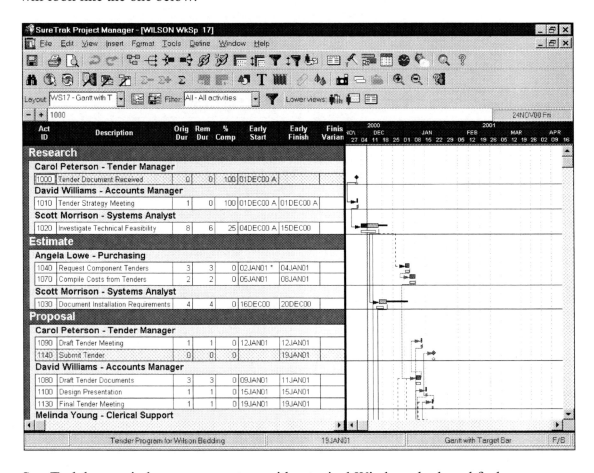 icon on the toolbar.

3.5   The Screen

After a project has been created from a template or opened using **File**, **Open** the screen will look like the one below:

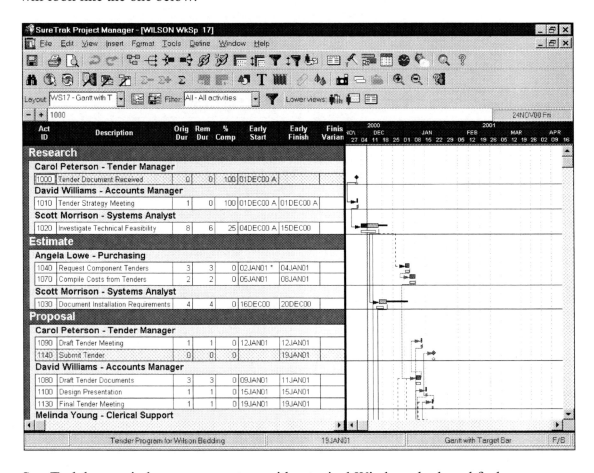

SureTrak has a windows menu system with a typical Windows look and feel.

- The project name is displayed in brackets after SureTrak Project Manager at the top of the screen.

- The pull-down menus are just below the project name.

- There are three toolbars that may be displayed below the menu. They are the **Tool Bar**, **Editing Toolbar** and **Layout Toolbar**. These may be displayed or hidden using the command **View** and clicking on **Toolbar**, **Editing Toolbar** or **Layout Toolbar**.

- The right-hand side of the line underneath the toolbars has the **Datometer**, the Datometer indicates the date at which the mouse is pointing.

- The left-hand side of the line underneath the toolbars has the **Edit Box**. The ▣ and ▤ icons are used for adding and deleting activities, and the ▨ and ▧ icons are used for accepting and not accepting data changes.

- The main display has the Bar Chart on the right-hand side and the Data Columns on the left-hand side with their titles above them.

- The Activity Form may be displayed or hidden by pressing **F7** or **View**, **Activity form**. More or less information is displayed in the Activity Form by using the ⬛ More >> and ⬛ << Less icons.

- At the bottom of the screen is the Status Bar. The content of the status bar may be customized, this topic is covered next.

3.6 Customizing the Screen

The screen may be customized in a number of ways to suit your preferences.

- The default font for the display may be changed using **Tools, Customize, Default Font**.

- There are three toolbars, Tool Bar, Editing Toolbar and Layout Toolbar. These may be edited by selecting **Tools, Customize, Toolbars**.

- The Status Bar may be edited to show different information by selecting **Tools, Customize, Status Bar**.

- The Language used in the column headers and the dates may be formatted by using **Tools, Customize, Set Language**.

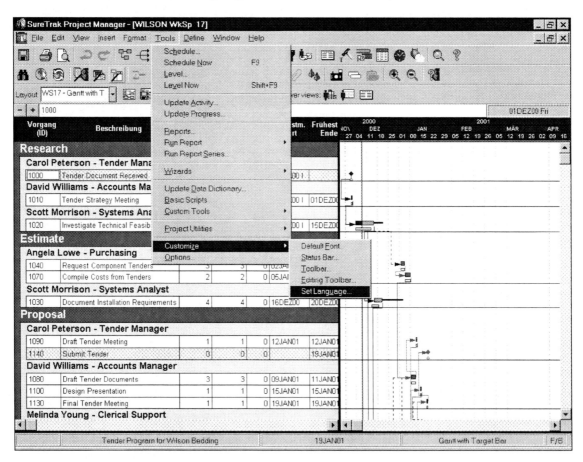

- The vertical split between the column area on the left and the bar area on the right may be moved by highlighting the dividing line to display a double arrow, hold down the left mouse button and dragging the dividing line to the left or right.

3.7 Setting up the Defaults

The basic parameters of the software must be configured so it will operate the way you desire. These configuration items may be found under **Tools, Options**.

Some of the defaults must be turned off or changed in order for the software to work and calculate in the way you want it to.

Select **Tools, Options** to display the **Options** form.

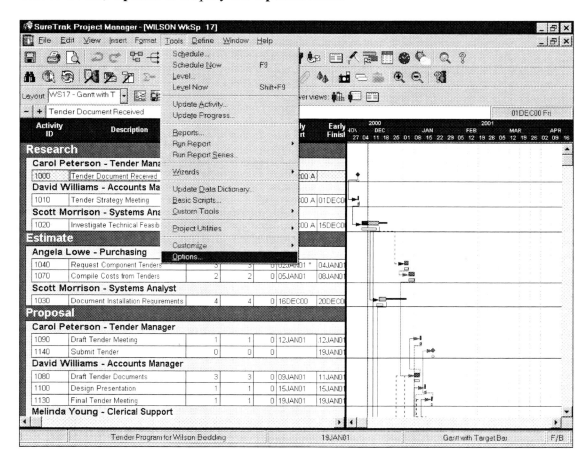

3.7.1   Options Form

Select the **Project** tab to display the form below. Most plans are scheduled in days, sometimes in days and hours, and occasionally in hours only. Select the options to meet your reporting requirements.

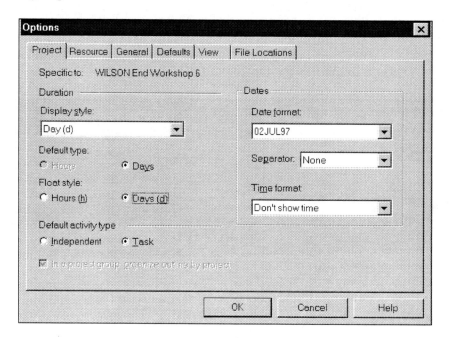

Below the **Duration** heading

- **Display style** is the format used to display durations in the Bar Chart columns. Select days unless more detailed planning is required.

- **Default type** specifies the format in which durations are entered via the keyboard. If **Day** is selected as the default then a duration of 2 days is entered as 2 (without the d) and a 2 hour duration should be entered as 2h, and vice versa if **Hours** are selected as **Default type**.

- **Float style** is the format displaying the float.

Default Activity Type

- This should be set as **Task** unless advanced resourcing calculations are required. These advanced options are covered in the **CREATING AND USING RESOURCES** and **USING ACTIVITY TYPES AND DRIVING RESOURCES** chapters.

Dates

- **Date format** is the format for date display.

- **Time format** is the format for the time display.

- **Separator** is to specify a separator between the day, month and year.

3.7.2   Schedule Form

Select **Tools, Schedule** to display the **Schedule** form.

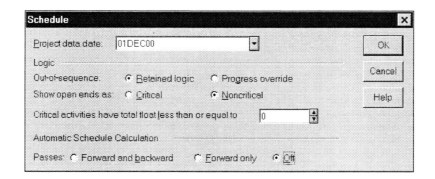

Project data date

- This is also known as the Status Date, As Of Date or the Update Date.

- This is the date from which all Early Start and Early Finish calculations are made.

- No unstarted or incomplete work will have the Early Start or Early Finish date scheduled before this date.

- This date is normally advanced on each schedule update.

- Press **F9** or select **Tools, Schedule** or click on the ⊕ icon to reschedule or calculate the project.

Logic

These options are discussed in the **TRACKING PROGRESS** chapter.

Automatic Schedule Calculation

Select **Automatic Schedule Calculation** if you do not want the software to calculate every time a change is made.

 It is often better to turn **Automatic Schedule Calculation** off when you are working on a large schedule. When it is left on SureTrak recalculates after every edit thus slowing you down while you wait for the software to recalculate.

WORKSHOP 2

Setting your Project Options

Preamble

For control purposes the minimum time for any activity will be set to one day. As the project has a fixed duration we will resource to meet the timeframes and, therefore, set our default activity type to **Task**.

Assignment

1. Set your project options to reflect those shown below.

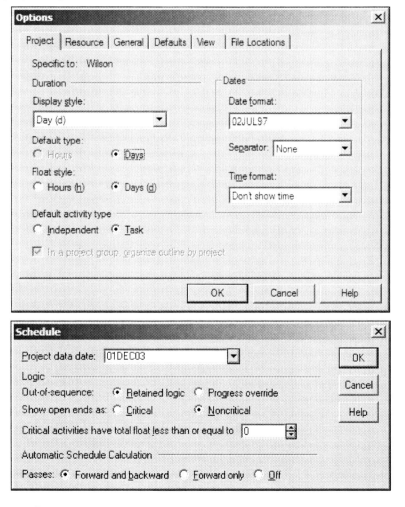

2. Save your project.

4 DEFINING CALENDARS

The end date of an activity is calculated from the start date plus the duration over the calendar associated with the activity. Therefore, a five day duration activity that starts on a Wednesday, and is associated with a five day work week calendar (with Saturday and Sunday as non-work days) will finish on the following Tuesday.

SureTrak has a Global Calendar and a minimum of one Base Calendar. The Global Calendar sets the default working days and hours used in new calendars and the holidays for all calendars.

The Global Calendar may not be assigned to an activity.

The Global Calendar may be edited for each new schedule.

Up to 31 Base calendars may be created. Base calendars are assigned to activities so as to allow for each activity's individual calendar requirements. For example, office work would be allocated a five-day calendar, while site work would be allocated a six-day calendar.

4.1 Global Calendar

Each Holiday or Non-workday nominated in the **Global Calendar** is reflected in all **Base calendars**. As a general rule you should make the Global Calendar 5 or 6 days per week at 8 hrs per day and include Public Holidays. Public Holidays on the same date every year may be made **Annual**. RDO's may also be entered here only if they affect all other calendars.

To edit, delete or create calendars select **Define**, **Calendars** to display the **Calendars** form. This will display the **Standard** tab as default

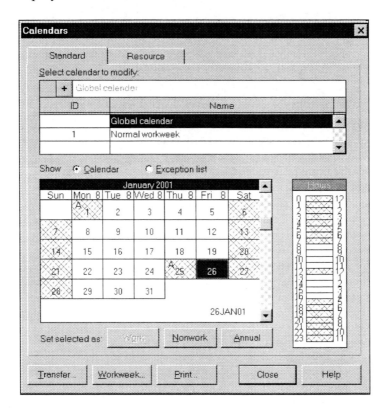

- Click on **Show Calendar** radio button to display the calendar or the **Show Exception list** radio button to see a complete list of holidays and non-work days.

- To make work days into holidays or **Nonwork** days, double click on the day or highlight the day and click on **Nonwork**.

- To make holidays or **Nonwork** days into working days double on them or highlight them and click on **Work**.

- Click on **Annual** to make the holiday apply every year.

- **Transfer** allows the transfer of calendars from another project.

Select **Workweek** to nominate the normal working days and hours.

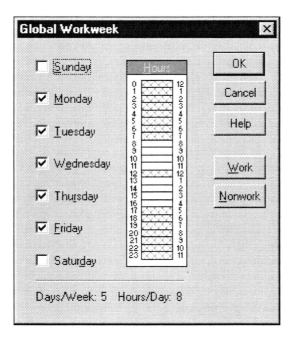

- Check the work days and work hours to reflect your standard working week.

- If the planning unit is days then do **not** change the hours for any day from 8 hours.

- Double click on the **Hours** to make each hour a **Work** or **Nonwork** period or highlight the [Work] or [Nonwork] icons.

 If it is intended to open a daily schedule in P3 then an 8-hour day calendar should be selected. This is because the task durations are divided by 8 when the project is opened in P3. If a project has a 10-hour day and is opened in P3 the durations will be increased by 25%.

4.2 Base Calendars

Up to 31 Base Calendars may be created and assigned to activities. Examples of other calendars are:

- 2 – Weekend only

- 3 – Three Shift/24hour per day

- 4 – Mon to Thu

- 5 – Day week

- 6 – Day week and

- 7 – Day week

Creating a New Calendar

- To create a new calendar click on the ▣ icon or select the first blank row in the list of calendars. Enter the ID and description.

- Holidays, work week and hours are changed using the same method as the Global Calendar.

- For simplicity, make the number of working hours the same for each day.

Deleting a Calendar

- Select the calendar and then click on the ▣ icon or strike the **Delete** key.

4.3 Resource Calendars

Individual Resources are allocated a base calendar when they are created. The resource calendar is edited to reflect the availability of the resource. This facility is covered in the **CREATING AND USING RESOURCES** chapter.

WORKSHOP 3

Maintaining the Calendars

Preamble

The normal working week at OzBuild Pty Ltd is Monday to Friday, 8 hours per day excluding Public Holidays. The installation staff work Monday to Saturday, 8 hours per day.

The company observes the following Australian holidays:

	2003	2004	2005
New Years Day	1 January	1 January	3 January*
Australia Day	27 January*	26 January	26 January
Good Friday	18 April	9 April	25 March
Easter	21 April	12 April	28 March
Anzac Day	25 April	26 April*	25 April
Queen's Birthday	9 June	14 June	13 June
Christmas Day	25 December	27 December*	26 December*
Boxing Day	26 December	28 December*	27 December*

Holidays with an * normally occur on a weekend and the date has been moved to the next weekday.

Assignment

1. Edit the Global Calendar to ensure only Australian holidays in 2003 and 2004 above are present. You may click on the Exception List radio button and delete any existing holidays. You may also wish to make Christmas Day, Boxing Day, New Years Day and Australia Day annual holidays, then add additional holidays for those that occur on a weekend.

2. Delete all calendars except Calendar ID 1.

3. Create calendar ID 5 for a five-day week and calendar ID 6 for the six-day week, these will both adopt holidays from the Global calendar.

4. Save your project.

5   ACTIVITY CODES

Activity codes are used to sort, select, summarize and group activities under headings. They are used to present different views of your project during planning, scheduling and statusing. These headings are often based on your Work Breakdown Structures (WBS) and Organization Breakdown Structure (OBS).

Defining the code structure can be a major task for project managers. The establishment of templates makes this simpler as your standard codes are then predefined and do not have to be typed in or transferred from another project.

Work Breakdown Structure

Projects should be broken up into manageable areas by using a Work Breakdown Structure or WBS. The WBS is usually based on a breakdown of the project deliverables.

SureTrak Activity Codes are created to reflect the breakdown or a project. A code would be created for each level in the WBS and values assigned to represent the components of the project. These values are then assigned to each activity allowing it to be grouped with other activities belonging to the same component.

Organization Breakdown Structure

Organization Breakdown Structure (OBS) is a term used to describe reporting hierarchy of people with areas of responsibility just like an organization chart within a company. Again, SureTrak Activity Codes are created for each level of the hierarchy and values assigned to reflect the various positions and roles. These values are then assigned to each activity for grouping together.

Other Breakdown Structures

Other common breakdown structures used are:

- Contract Breakdown Structure – allocating activities to contracts;

- System Breakdown Structure – breaking a System into Sub-systems and Sub-sub-systems as used in System Engineering;

- Area Breakdown – that breaks the project down into physical areas or locations.

5.1 Defining Activity Codes

Select **Define**, **Activity Codes** to display the **Activity Codes** form.

- **Transfer** allows you to transfer codes from another project.

SureTrak has two types of activity codes: **Activity Codes** and **Activity ID Codes**.

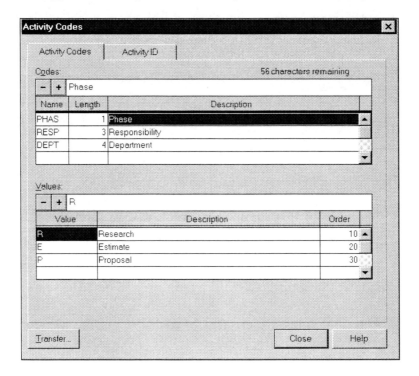

- **Activity Codes** are assigned to activities in the **Activity Task** form or using other methods.

- **Activity ID Codes** are assigned through the logical coding of the Activity ID. These are discussed in the **ORGANISING ACTIVITIES** chapter.

An **Activity Code** has a **Name**, a **Length** and a **Description**. The Dictionary holds a series of **Values** and each **Value** has a **Description** and an **Order**. In the example above:

- The dictionary for the **Phases** of the Project is named **PHAS**

- R is the code for the Research

- E is the code for the Estimation

- P is the code for the Proposal.

5.2 Creating and Deleting Code Dictionaries

Select the ⊞ icon under the title **Codes** to create a new Code Dictionary and select the ⊟ icon to delete the dictionary, including all codes.

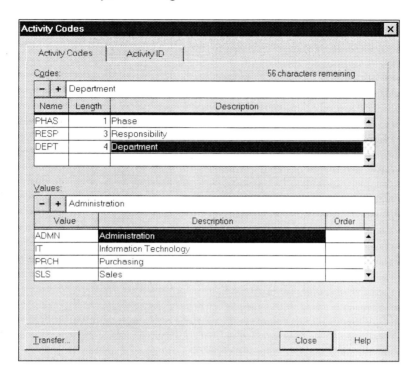

- Give the dictionary **Name** of up to four characters.

- Nominate a **Length** to a maximum of 10 characters. The length is the maximum number of characters the code may have. Type in the **Description** for the code.

- A maximum length of 64 characters for all the Code Lengths added together is permitted.

- A maximum of 20 **Codes** are permitted.

 The code is typed into a column or box to allocate the code to an activity. It is recommended that you keep the code length as short as possible to reduce the number of key strokes when assigning codes against activities.

5.3   Creating and Deleting Activity Codes

In the lower window of the **Activity Codes** form.

- Click on the ▣ in the lower window or click into the first blank line to create a new code.

- Allocate the code **Value**. The maximum length is the code **Length** nominated in the upper window. Use uppercase characters and numbers only.

- Type in the **Description** of the code.

- Allocate the **Order**, from 1 to 254 to order the Codes on the screen. If the order is not used (or has the same value) then the codes will be displayed alphabetically.

- Select the ▣ icon to delete a code.

WORKSHOP 4

Maintaining the Activity Codes

Preamble

A review of the internal reporting requirements show that you need to identify the:

Work Phase –
Research
Estimation
Proposal

Person Responsible –
Angela Lowe   Purchasing
Carol Peterson   Bid Manager
David Williams   Account Manager
Melinda Young   Clerical Support
Scott Morrison   Systems Analyst

Department –
Sales
Purchasing
Information Technology
Administration

Assignment

1. In the table on the next page write down the dictionary names, lengths and descriptions and then the activity code, values and descriptions you would create from the information above.

2. Delete any existing Activity Code dictionaries that are not required and then create the Activity Code dictionaries and Activity Codes using the details on page 5-8.

FIRST CODE DICTIONARY

Name	Length	Description

FIRST DICTIONARY CODES

Value	Description	Order

SECOND CODE DICTIONARY

Name	Length	Description

SECOND DICTIONARY CODES

Value	Description	Order

THIRD CODE DICTIONARY

Name	Length	Description

THIRD DICTIONARY CODES

Value	Description	Order

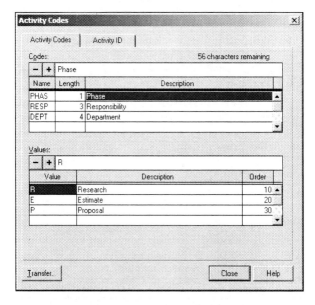

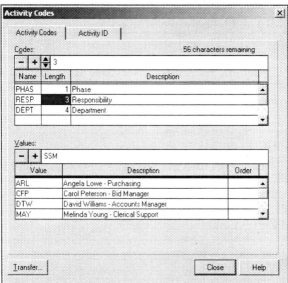

AND ADD Scott Morrison – Systems Analyst as SSM

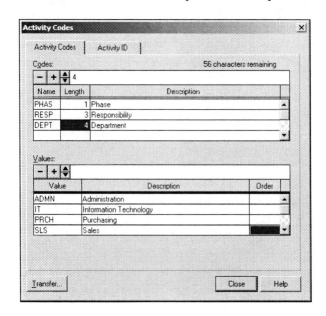

6   ADDING ACTIVITIES

Activities should be well defined and measurable pieces of work with a measurable outcome. Activities such as "Slab" have confusing meanings. Does this mean form up, inspect, pour, fix reo, cure or all of these? A more appropriate activity would be "Pour Slab" or maybe "Install & Cure Slab". It also helps to repeat the code title in the activity description (ie: "Install & Cure Slab First Floor" if you have room). The limit for the descriptions is 48 characters so try to keep the activity descriptions brief but meaningful.

6.1   Adding New Activities

There are several methods to add a task or activity.

Method 1

The first and easiest is to click on the plus sign toward the top left of the screen. Press **F7** to access the Activity Form or select **View**, **Activity Form**.

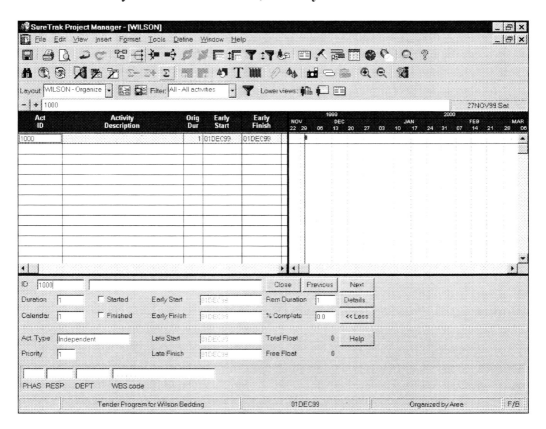

- In the **Activity Form**, accept the SureTrak Activity **ID** or replace it with your own.

- **Tab** and enter the **Description**.

- **Tab** and enter the **Duration**.

- **Tab** and assign the calendar if Calendar 1 is not correct.

- The Remaining Duration (**Rem Dur**) will default to the original duration.

Method 2

The second method of adding an activity is to just click on the area below the existing activities. SureTrak will automatically create an activity for you.

Method 3

The third method is to select **Insert**, **Activity** or press the **Ins** (insert) key on the keyboard.

6.2 Copying Activities in SureTrak

Activities may also be copied from another project or copied from within the same project, using the normal Windows commands **Copy** and **Paste**. These commands are also executed by using the menu commands **Edit Copy** and **Edit Paste** or **Ctrl C** and **Ctrl V**.

The **Paste Options** form will be displayed to give you options for creating new Activity ID's.

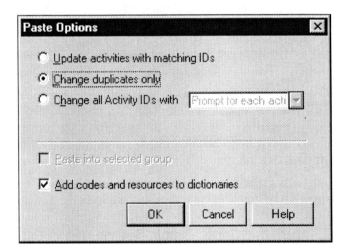

6.3 Copying Activities from other Programs

Most of the activity data may be copied to and from or updated from other programs such as Excel by cutting and pasting. The Activity ID must be included. It is recommended to copy one activity in SureTrak whilst displaying the required column headings and paste it into Excel. This also copies in the necessary headings from SureTrak. Arrange the new data in Excel and Cut and Paste the new activities back into SureTrak. Some data may not be pasted such as Constraint types and Resource Cost and Quantities but Dates Durations, Percentage Complete and Activity Codes will.

6.4 Activity Types

Activities are assigned a **Type** to enable schedulers to more closely simulate real life situations. SureTrak has a number of Activity Types that will be covered in detail in the chapter **USING ACTIVITY TYPES AND DRIVING RESOURCES**. These are the three most commonly used types.

Task

An activity is nominated as a Task when it has a Start Date, a Duration and a Finish Date and is used for most activities.

Start Milestone

An activity is nominated as a Start Milestone when it has a Start Date only. It has no Duration or Finish Date and is normally used to mark the start of a major event.

Finish Milestone

An activity is assigned as a Finish Milestone when it has a Finish Date only. It has no duration or start date and is normally used to mark the end of a major event.

6.5 Assigning Activity Type to an Activity

Activity Types may be assigned by:

- Selecting the Activity Type from the **Act. Type** drop-down box in the **Activity** form or typing in the first letter of the Type in the **Act. Type** drop-down box.

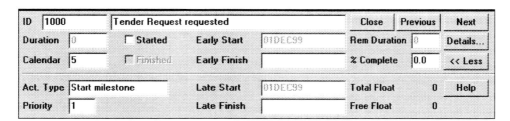

- Displaying a column with Activity Type and updating the column.

WORKSHOP 5

Adding Activities

Preamble

Having set up the activity codes you may begin entering the activities.

Assignment

1. Use the **Activity** form to enter the activities, Original Duration, Calendar and Type as detailed below. Note: Do not format the columns as per the diagram.

Act ID	Description	Orig Dur	Calendar	Activity Type
1000	Bid Request Documents Received	0	5	Start
1010	Bid Strategy Meeting	1	5	Task
1020	Investigate Technical Feasibility	8	5	Task
1030	Document Installation Requirements	4	6	Task
1040	Request Component Tenders	3	5	Task
1050	Develop Project Schedule	4	6	Task
1060	Draft Technical Details Schedule	9	5	Task
1070	Compile Costs from Component Bids	2	5	Task
1080	Draft the Bid Document	3	5	Task
1090	Meeting to review the Draft Bid	1	5	Task
1100	Design Presentation	1	5	Task
1110	Edit Proposal Draft Bid Document	1	5	Task
1120	Negotiate Component Work Packages	6	5	Task
1130	Final Review of Bid Document	1	5	Task
1140	Submit Bid	0	5	Finish

2. Save your project.

7   FORMATTING THE DISPLAY

Set up the on-screen presentation so that the schedule is easy to read and consistent. This chapter covers the following customizing topics:

- Columns

- Bar Chart

- Row Height

- Screen Colors

- Timescale

- Sightlines

7.1   Formatting Columns

Formatting columns allows you to set up the columns you wish to see on the screen and in printouts. Select **Format, Columns** or double click on the column headings or click the ▦ icon on the toolbar to display the **Format** form below.

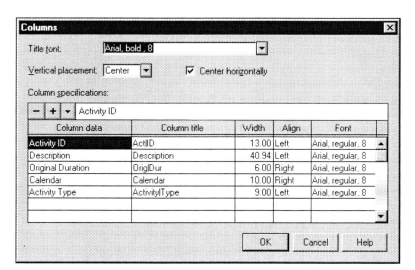

- The columns to be displayed are listed under **Column data** and appear from left to right on the screen.

- Use the ⊞ and ⊟ under **Column specifications** to insert or delete columns.

- The **Column title** allows the title to be customized. Use the pipe symbol | (usually uppercase \) to force a new line in the title.

- Use **Width, Align** and **Font** to format the data in the columns.

- The column titles are formatted using the options in the upper box.

- To change the order of **Column data** in the **Column specifications**, then click on the data item you wish to move, hold down the **Ctrl** key, left click with the mouse and drag to a new position. This function works with many other forms.

WORKSHOP 6

Tailoring your Columns

Preamble

You need to produce a report to confirm your data entry.

Assignment

1. Required fields are:

    - Activity ID

    - Description

    - Original Duration

    - Calendar

    - Activity Type

2. Format your columns to reflect the output below.

Act ID	Description	Orig Dur	Calendar	Activity Type
1000	Bid Request Documents Received	0	5	Start
1010	Bid Strategy Meeting	1	5	Task
1020	Investigate Technical Feasibility	8	5	Task
1030	Document Installation Requirements	4	6	Task
1040	Request Component Tenders	3	5	Task
1050	Develop Project Schedule	4	6	Task
1060	Draft Technical Details Schedule	9	5	Task
1070	Compile Costs from Component Bids	2	5	Task
1080	Draft the Bid Document	3	5	Task
1090	Meeting to review the Draft Bid	1	5	Task
1100	Design Presentation	1	5	Task
1110	Edit Proposal Draft Bid Document	1	5	Task
1120	Negotiate Component Work Packages	6	5	Task
1130	Final Review of Bid Document	1	5	Task
1140	Submit Bid	0	5	Finish

7.2 Formatting the Bars in the Bar Chart

To format bars and end points on the bar chart you will need to select each bar or point in turn from the list in the **Format Bars** form and format them by selecting attributes such as size and color. For clarity it is recommended that the Bars are formatted as shown below.

Select **Format**, **Bars** or click the ▦ icon on the toolbar to display the **Format Bars** form.

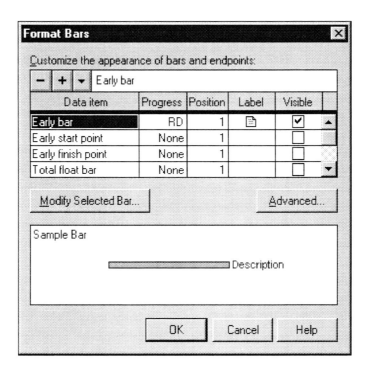

Under **Data item** add or delete a bar or point using the ⊡ or ⊟ icons.

- Under **Data item** select the bar or point you wish to work with.

- **Progress** displays the progress on the bar. There are three options:
  - ➢ **None** does not display progress on the bar,
  - ➢ **RD** displays the Remaining Duration and
  - ➢ **PCT** displays the % Complete on the bar.

- **Position** determines vertical placement. Position 1 is displayed above position 2.

- Click on the **Label** box to open the **Label Text** form, this is for adding text by bars and **Text Separator** nominates the separator between data in the same position.

- **Visible** allows bars to be formatted but not displayed.

- Modify Selected Bar opens the Modify Bar Elements form covered next.

- Advanced opens the Format Bars Advanced form covered next.

7.2.1   Modify Selected Bar

This function allows you to modify one or more selected bars with color and style formatting.

Select one or more bars that require special formatting.

Then to open the Modify Bar Elements form select either:

- Format, Bars, Modify Selected Bar… or

- **Format, Selected Bars, Modify**

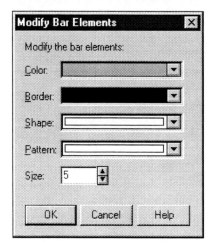

- **Color**, **Border**, **Shape** and **Pattern** are used to format the bars and points.

- **Size** determines the height of the bar or point.

The formatting may be copied and pasted to other bars and changed back to the standard format using the commands under **Format, Selected Bars**.

7.2.2   Format Bars-Advanced

This allows you an additional selection of style colors and pattern for the bars in the Bar Chart. Select **Advanced** in the **Format Bar** form to open the **Format Bars Advanced** form.

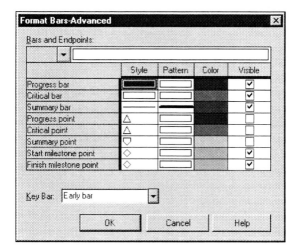

- A bar is displayed on the Bar Chart when it is **Visible** and is deleted from the Bar Key on printouts when it is not **Visible**.

- **Key Bar**. One bar is nominated the key bar. This bar is used for manipulating the activities in the Bar Chart area, such as adding logic and dragging to increase durations. The **Key Bar** must be displayed to graphically manipulate data such as adding logic.

7.3 Row Height

Row heights may be adjusted to display text that would otherwise be truncated by a narrow column.

The row height may be adjusted by selecting **Format**, **Row Height** to display the **Row Height** form.

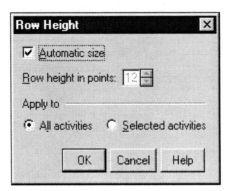

You may also adjust the height of a row by dragging with the mouse. Highlight one or more rows that need adjusting. Then move the mouse pointer to a horizontal row divider line then the pointer will change to a double headed arrow ↕ . Click with the left mouse button and drag the row or rows to the required height.

7.4   Screen Colors

The Screen Colors formatting only applies to some of the colors on the screen. Band colors are formatted in Organize.

The dark background with light printing is unsatisfactory on some black and white printers so you may need to choose a more acceptable screen color scheme.

Select **Format**, **Screen Colors** or click the ⊼ icon on the toolbar to display the **Screen Color** form.

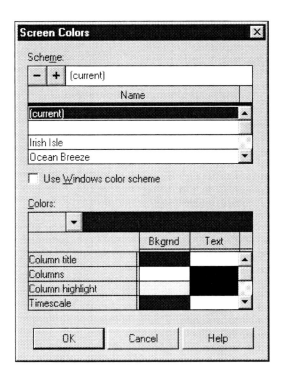

There are a number of standard color schemes available to choose from or you may create your own.

- Select the ⊞ icon to create your own.

- Select the ⊟ icon to delete one you do not require.

- Click **Use Windows color scheme** to use the current Windows scheme on your schedule.

7.5 Format Timescale

Format Timescale provides a number of options for formatting the timescale displayed above the Bar Chart. The Format Timescale Form also includes a Tab to the Format Sightlines Form. Format Sightlines is outlined in Section 7.6.

SureTrak has a very useful feature to prevent the right hand boundary of the Bar Chart from scrolling outside predefined dates and "becoming lost" in the past or future. The setting of the **Begin date** and **End date** prevents you from scrolling out of the project time span.

Select **Format, Timescale** to display the **Timescale** form.

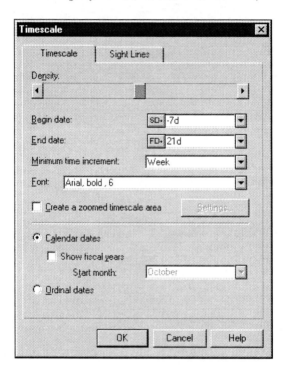

- Click on the box in the slide below **Density** and slide the box left and right to alter the scale of the displayed time scale.

- **Begin date** and **End date** options stop the left-hand side of the Bar Chart from scrolling outside this date plus or minus the number of days entered in the box. You should set the **Timescale** to a scale that best suits your needs. A good starting point is to set the **Begin date** at **Data Date –10 days** and the **End date** at **Finish Date +10 days**.

- **Minimum time increment** is the smallest time increment to be displayed: hours, days, weeks, months, quarters or years. Typical, the minimum time increment to display on screen is to a **Week**.

- **Font** specifies the font for the timescale.

- **Create a zoomed timescale area** opens a new form which allows the timescale to be zoomed into a smaller area than the entire project timescale. See Chapter 20 for more details.

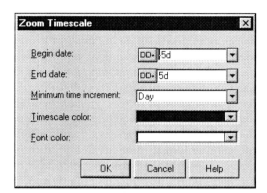

- **Calendar dates, Show fiscal years** displays accounting style years, with the first month being something other than January (this is often set to June).

- **Ordinal dates** counts in days, weeks or months from the **Project Start Date**. This is useful for reporting project durations when you do not know the project start date.

There are two methods to set the **Begin date** and **End date** of the Timescale.

Method 1

- Click on the box to the right of **Begin date** and/or **End date** and select either Start Date, Data Date or End date.

- Enter the number of days in the box to the right of the **Begin date** or **End date** to set the final Begin date or End date.

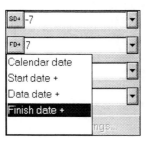

Method 2

Click on the box to the right of **Begin date** and/or **End date** and select **CAL** then click on the down arrow to the right and select a calendar date.

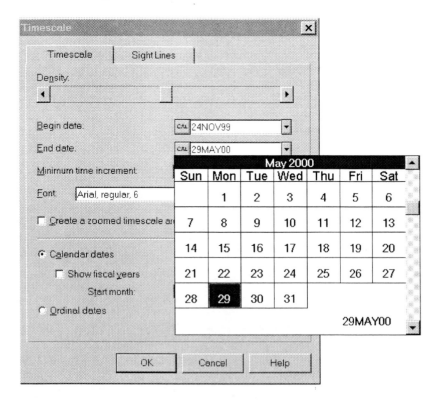

Minimum time increment may also be set by double clicking in the top of the Timescale, where the years are displayed in the Bar Chart, and continuing to double click to scroll through the options.

7.6   Format Sight Lines

Sight Lines are important to help divide the visual presentation of the dividing lines on the Bar Chart. This example shows **Major Sight Lines** every month and **Minor Sight Lines** every week.

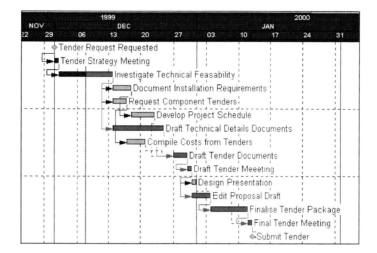

Select **Format**, **Sight Lines** to display the **Sight Line** form or select the **Sight Lines** Tab from the **Format**, **Timescale** Form. Use this form to format Bar Chart Horizontal and Vertical Sight Lines in the bar area and the Sight Lines in the column area.

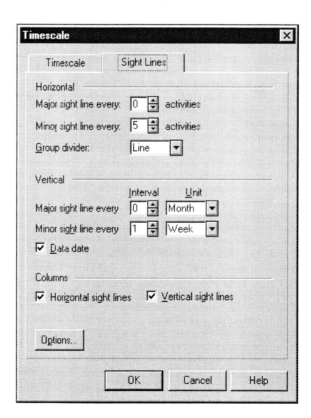

- Uncheck the **Data date** box to hide the data date.

- Uncheck the **Horizontal sight lines** and **Vertical sight lines** boxes to hide the dividing lines in the column area.

- Select **Options** to open the **Sight Line Options** form to format the Sight Line type and colors.

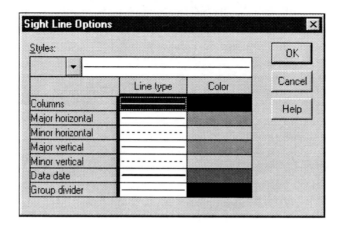

 Many laser printers will not print out light grey so it is often better to use dark grey or black Sight Lines.

7.7 Format Relationship Lines

Select **Format**, **Relationship Lines** to open the **Format Relationship Lines** form.

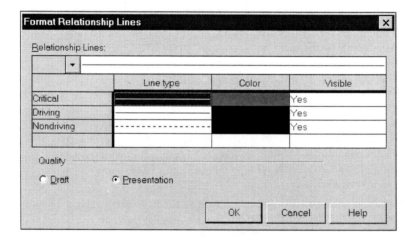

- **Draft Quality** draws the lines more quickly as shared lines are drawn but this makes tracing logic more difficult.

- **Visible** allows lines to be hidden.

WORKSHOP 7

Formatting the Bar Chart

Preamble

Management have received your draft report and requested some changes to the presentation.

Assignment

Format the report to reflect the report below by:

1. Formatting the timescale to days.

2. Set Major sight lines to monthly and Minor to weekly.

3. Hide the end points on the bars if displayed and display the end points if they are hidden.

4. Remove the activity descriptions from the bars.

5. Set the progress on the Early bar set to Percent Complete.

6. Replace Calendar and Activity Type columns with Early Start and Early Finish columns.

7. Save your project.

Act ID	Description	Orig Dur	Early Start	Early Finish	NOV 30	01	02	03	04	05	06	DEC 07	08	09	10	11	12
1000	Bid Request Documents Received	0	01DEC03														
1010	Bid Strategy Meeting	1	01DEC03	01DEC03													
1020	Investigate Technical Feasibility	8	01DEC03	10DEC03													
1030	Document Installation Requirements	4	01DEC03	04DEC03													
1040	Request Component Tenders	3	01DEC03	03DEC03													
1050	Develop Project Schedule	4	01DEC03	04DEC03													
1060	Draft Technical Details Schedule	9	01DEC03	11DEC03													
1070	Compile Costs from Component Bids	2	01DEC03	02DEC03													
1080	Draft the Bid Document	3	01DEC03	03DEC03													
1090	Meeting to review the Draft Bid	1	01DEC03	01DEC03													
1100	Design Presentation	1	01DEC03	01DEC03													
1110	Edit Proposal Draft Bid Document	1	01DEC03	01DEC03													
1120	Negotiate Component Work Packages	6	01DEC03	08DEC03													
1130	Final Review of Bid Document	1	01DEC03	01DEC03													
1140	Submit Bid	0		28NOV03													

8   ASSIGNING ACTIVITY CODES AND ORGANIZING

Activities are assigned **Activity Codes**. Then activities may be grouped and sorted under these codes, enabling the same information to be presented in a number of different formats.

Activity Codes must be assigned to activities before the activities may be grouped under their code. The activities are then sorted under their respective Activity Code headings using **Organize**.

The example below shows a project organized by **Phase** and **Responsibility**. Phase headings, such as **Research** and **Estimate**, are shown in **Bands**, with their associated activities below them. Activities under bands may be summarized, with their activities hidden. These have a "+" in front of the band heading and a summary bar representing all the activities in the bar area.

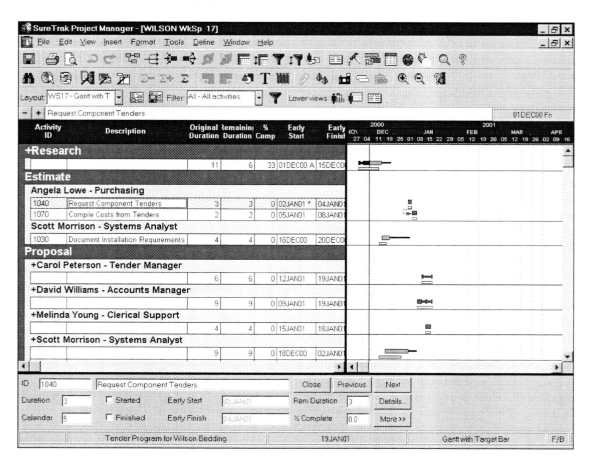

The bands are summarized by:

- Double clicking on the band

- Selecting Format, Summarization or

- Using the **Summarize** icons on the toolbar

8.1 Assigning Activity Codes

You may assign Activity Codes to activities as you create them or you may assign the codes at a later date. Activity Codes may be assigned or changed by either:

- Using the Activity Code boxes at the bottom of the **Task** form (F7)

- Creating a column for each code dictionary and assigning the codes in the column using the edit box or **Copy cell** and **Paste cell**

- Using the **Codes** form by selecting **View**, **Activity Detail**

- Click on an Activity, hold down the left button and drag the activity into the required band. This will assign the Activity Code of the band it is dragged into.

- A new activity will adopt the Activity Codes that are displayed in the current layout assigned to the activity that is highlighted when the activity is created.

As new activities are created in a band, the software assumes the same code for each new activity as the band in which they are created.

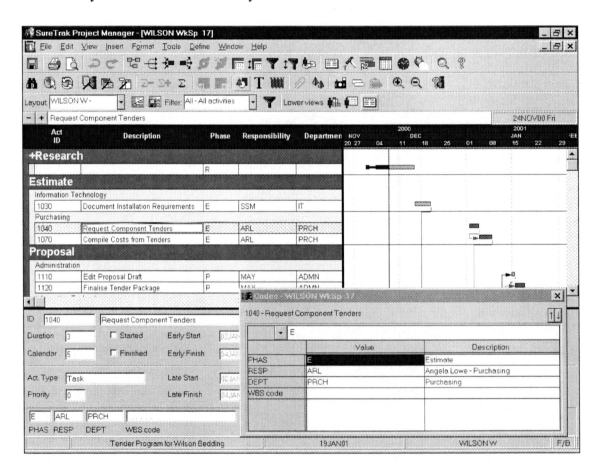

The above example shows:

- Activities grouped by Phase and Department
- The **Codes** form
- Codes at the bottom of the **Task** form
- Codes displayed in columns

You may create new codes as you enter activities and return to the activity code dictionary later, by selecting **Define**, **Activity Codes**, to add the Description.

 If you delete a value from an activity code the software will automatically remove it from all activities that it has been assigned.

WORKSHOP 8

Assigning Activity Codes

Preamble

Having entered the activities you may now assign the codes.

Assignment

1. Format your columns to reflect details below.

Act ID	Description	Orig Dur	Early Start	Early Finish	Phase	Responsibility	Department
1000	Bid Request Documents Received	0	01DEC03		R	CFP	SLS
1010	Bid Strategy Meeting	1	01DEC03	01DEC03	R	DTW	PRCH
1020	Investigate Technical Feasibility	8	01DEC03	10DEC03	R	SSM	IT
1030	Document Installation Requirements	4	01DEC03	04DEC03	E	SSM	IT
1040	Request Component Tenders	3	01DEC03	03DEC03	E	ARL	PRCH
1050	Develop Project Schedule	4	01DEC03	04DEC03	P	SSM	IT
1060	Draft Technical Details Schedule	9	01DEC03	11DEC03	P	SSM	IT
1070	Compile Costs from Component Bids	2	01DEC03	02DEC03	E	ARL	PRCH
1080	Draft the Bid Document	3	01DEC03	03DEC03	P	DTW	PRCH
1090	Meeting to review the Draft Bid	1	01DEC03	01DEC03	P	CFP	SLS
1100	Design Presentation	1	01DEC03	01DEC03	P	DTW	PRCH
1110	Edit Proposal Draft Bid Document	1	01DEC03	01DEC03	P	MAY	ADMN
1120	Negotiate Component Work Packages	6	01DEC03	08DEC03	P	MAY	ADMN
1130	Final Review of Bid Document	1	01DEC03	01DEC03	P	DTW	PRCH
1140	Submit Bid	0		28NOV03	P	CFP	SLS

2. Try using all the methods outlined in the chapter to assign these codes.

3. Save your project.

8.2 Organizing Activities

Projects may be organized by Activity Codes and many other Activity Data Items such as resources, dates, float, percentages, predecessors and successors. Select **Format, Organize** or click the ▦ icon on the toolbar to display the **Organize** form.

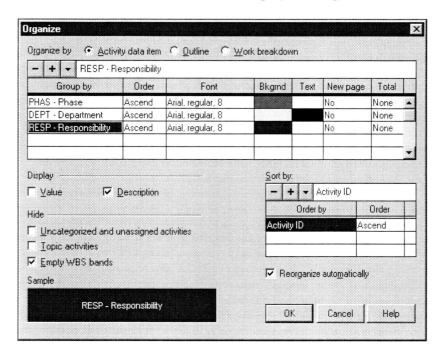

- Select the **Activity data item** radio button.

- In the upper window of the form click on the ⊡ icon to create or the ⊡ icon to delete the **Activity Code** or data item you wish to summarize the activities under.

- Use **Order, Font, Bkgnd** (Background) and **Text** to format the headings.

- **New Page** creates a page break at each new Group Code when printing.

- **Total** places a total at the top or bottom of a group. Values and Quantities are totaled in the band created by **Organize**. Dates are calculated as the minimum of all start dates and maximum of end dates in a group.

- **Sort by** is used to order the activities within bands.

- Check the following boxes under **Display**:

- **Value** to display the Activity Code value in the group band or

- **Description** to display the code description in the group band.

- Check the following boxes under **Hide**:

- **Uncategorized and unassigned activities** to display activities without codes selected in **Organize**. These are displayed in a band without a title.

- **Topic Activities** hides Topic Activities. These **Summary Activities** which are normally created in Microsoft Project and may be created and used in SureTrak.

- **Empty WBS bands** will not display WBS bands defined in WBS codes that have not been assigned an activity.

- When **Reorganize automatically** is switched off you may reorganize the activities after assigning or changing Activity Codes by pressing **F5** or selecting **Format, Reorganize** or clicking the icon on the toolbar.

 The **Reorganize** function moves activities under their correct group headings when a code is assigned or changed. It is recommended that you switch off this facility when you assign Activity Codes to prevent activities from moving around at each code assignment.

WORKSHOP 9

Organizing your Data

Preamble

Having entered the activity codes you may report the information with═ different layouts.

Assignment

Try organizing your project as follows, noting the different ways you may represent the same data.

1. Display the Early Start and Early Finish columns between Description and Phase.

2. Group by Phase and sort by Description.

Act ID	Description	Orig Dur	Early Start	Early Finish	Phase	Responsibility	Department
Research							
1000	Bid Request Documents Received	0	01DEC03		R	CFP	SLS
1010	Bid Strategy Meeting	1	01DEC03	01DEC03	R	DTW	PRCH
1020	Investigate Technical Feasibility	8	01DEC03	10DEC03	R	SSM	IT
Estimate							
1070	Compile Costs from Component Bids	2	01DEC03	02DEC03	E	ARL	PRCH
1030	Document Installation Requirements	4	01DEC03	04DEC03	E	SSM	IT
1040	Request Component Tenders	3	01DEC03	03DEC03	E	ARL	PRCH
Proposal							
1100	Design Presentation	1	01DEC03	01DEC03	P	DTW	PRCH
1050	Develop Project Schedule	4	01DEC03	04DEC03	P	SSM	IT
1060	Draft Technical Details Schedule	9	01DEC03	11DEC03	P	SSM	IT
1080	Draft the Bid Document	3	01DEC03	03DEC03	P	DTW	PRCH
1110	Edit Proposal Draft Bid Document	1	01DEC03	01DEC03	P	MAY	ADMN
1130	Final Review of Bid Document	1	01DEC03	01DEC03	P	DTW	PRCH
1090	Meeting to review the Draft Bid	1	01DEC03	01DEC03	P	CFP	SLS
1120	Negotiate Component Work Packages	6	01DEC03	08DEC03	P	MAY	ADMN
1140	Submit Bid	0		28NOV03	P	CFP	SLS

3. Remove grouping and group by Department, Responsibility and Phase.

Act ID	Description	Orig Dur	Early Start	Early Finish	Phase	Responsibility	Department
Administration							
Melinda Young - Clerical Support							
Proposal							
1110	Edit Proposal Draft Bid Document	1	01DEC03	01DEC03	P	MAY	ADMN
1120	Negotiate Component Work Packages	6	01DEC03	08DEC03	P	MAY	ADMN
Information Technology							
Scott Morrison - Systems Analyst							
Research							
1020	Investigate Technical Feasibility	8	01DEC03	10DEC03	R	SSM	IT
Estimate							
1030	Document Installation Requirements	4	01DEC03	04DEC03	E	SSM	IT
Proposal							
1050	Develop Project Schedule	4	01DEC03	04DEC03	P	SSM	IT
1060	Draft Technical Details Schedule	9	01DEC03	11DEC03	P	SSM	IT
Purchasing							
Angela Lowe - Purchasing							
Estimate							
1070	Compile Costs from Component Bids	2	01DEC03	02DEC03	E	ARL	PRCH
1040	Request Component Tenders	3	01DEC03	03DEC03	E	ARL	PRCH

4. Total the Responsibility Grouping only – place it at the top.

Act ID	Description	Orig Dur	Early Start	Early Finish	Phase	Responsibility	Department
Administration							
Melinda Young - Clerical Support							
		6	01DEC03	08DEC03	P	MAY	ADMN
Proposal							
1110	Edit Proposal Draft Bid Document	1	01DEC03	01DEC03	P	MAY	ADMN
1120	Negotiate Component Work Packages	6	01DEC03	08DEC03	P	MAY	ADMN
Information Technology							
Scott Morrison - Systems Analyst							
		9	01DEC03	11DEC03		SSM	IT
Research							
1020	Investigate Technical Feasibility	8	01DEC03	10DEC03	R	SSM	IT
Estimate							
1030	Document Installation Requirements	4	01DEC03	04DEC03	E	SSM	IT
Proposal							
1050	Develop Project Schedule	4	01DEC03	04DEC03	P	SSM	IT
1060	Draft Technical Details Schedule	9	01DEC03	11DEC03	P	SSM	IT

5. Remove all grouping and sort by Activity ID.

6. Save your project.

9   ADDING THE LOGIC

The next phase of a schedule is to add logic to the activities. There are two types of logic that you must deal with here:

- **Logic links** or **relationships** between activities and

- Imposed **constraints** to the activities.

9.1   Understanding Relationships

There are four types of relationship available in SureTrak:

- Finish-to-Start (**FS**) (also known as conventional)

- Start-to-Start (**SS**)

- Start-to-Finish (**SF)**

- Finish-to-Finish (**FF)**

Two other terms you must understand are:

- **Predecessor**, an activity that controls the start or finish of another activity and

- **Successor**, an activity whose start or finish depends on the start or finish of another activity.

The **FS** (or conventional) relationship looks like this:

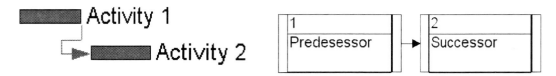

While the **SS** relationship is like this:

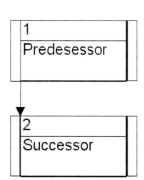

The **SF** relationship looks like:

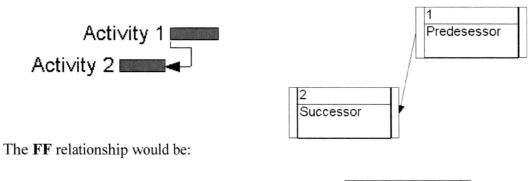

The **FF** relationship would be:

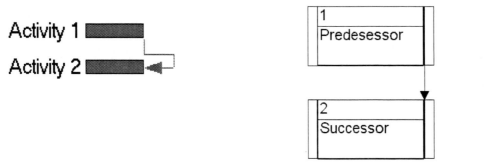

An example of a **FS** with positive lag:

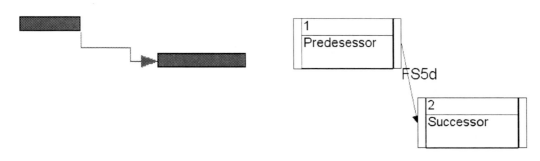

and an example of a **FS** with negative lag:

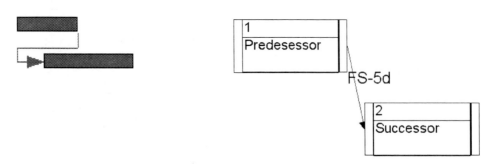

> ℹ️ You must be careful when using a lag to allow for delays such as curing concrete when the predecessor is not a seven-day calendar. The concrete will cure while the predecessor calendar has non-work days, and therefore, may be cured before SureTrak's allotted date.

9.2 Adding Relationships to the Activities

There are a number of methods of adding logic to activities. We will look at the following techniques:

- Graphical Adding, Editing and Deleting Relationships
- Series Link and Unlink
- Successor and Predecessor forms
- PERT View

9.2.1 Graphical Adding Relationships

There are two modes of screen presentation. The first is with links displayed on the screen and the second is without links. Logic may be added on the screen using the mouse when links are displayed or hidden. To change between modes click on the ▣ icon in the tool bar, push **F3** or select **View, Relationships**.

The **Relationship Lines** may be formatted by selecting **Format, Relationship Lines** which will display the **Format Relationship Lines** form. The defaults are normally acceptable.

To add relationships you can click on the end of the predecessor activity bar, which will change the mouse arrow to a ⤳. Then simply hold down the left mouse, drag to the start of the successor activity and release the mouse button.

To create other relationships such as **Start to Start**, drag from the beginning of the predecessor to the beginning of the successor bar.

When you add a link, SureTrak will display the **Successor Activity** form, to confirm the link, the type of link and the lag.

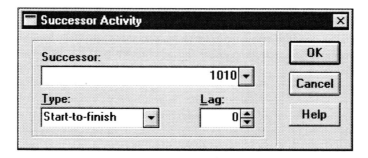

9.2.2   Editing Relationships in the Bar Chart View

To edit a relationship, move the mouse arrow over the relationship line to display the 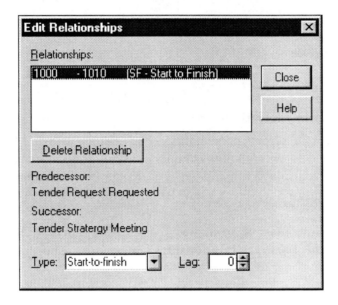 icon. Right click to display the **Edit Relationships** form where you will be able to select and edit or delete a relationship.

9.2.3   Series Link and Unlink

The Series Link is a method of linking a series of activities with **Finish to Start** relationships. To series link activities:

- Highlight the activities that are to be linked

- Click **Edit**, **Link Activities**, **F8** or the icon on the tool bar

- All the activities are now linked

The activities need not be consecutive activities to be **Series Linked**. Activities may be selected at random with the **Ctrl** key held down and then **Series Linked**. When activities lower down in the schedule are selected first they will not be linked in the order they were selected. Activities will be linked from top to bottom.

To remove Finish to Start relationships, highlight the activities to be unlinked and select:

- The icon on the tool bar or

- Select **Edit**, **Unlink** or

- Press Shift F8

9.2.4   Successor and Predecessor Forms

The third way to link activities is to use the **Successor** and the **Predecessor** form associated with each activity. There are two methods of opening these forms.

Method 1

- Highlight the activity then click the right mouse button to display a menu.

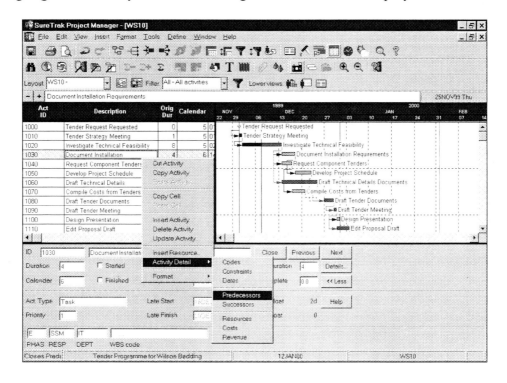

- Select **Activity Detail**, and a second menu is displayed.

- Select the form you wish to use. The **Predecessor** form is shown below.

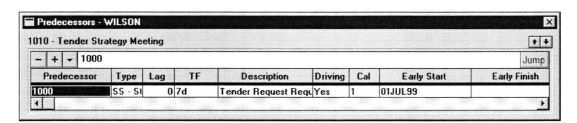

- You may add, delete or edit the relationships, including the link type and the lag.

- **Jump** takes you to the activity that is highlighted in the form to assist you in tracing the logic.

Method 2

Select **View**, **Activity Detail** to display the same menu that the right mouse button displays. Select the form you wish to use.

9.3 PERT View

The last method is to use PERT (Project Evaluation and Review Technique) view. This is a non-time phased view of the activities. Select **View, PERT** or press **F6**. The screen will change from Bar Chart view to PERT view.

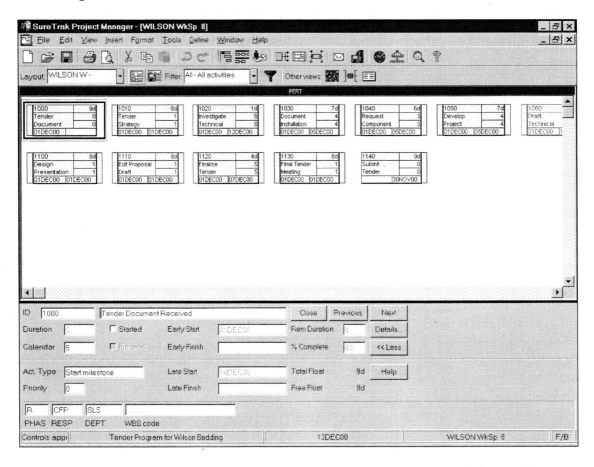

Position the mouse on the left (for start) or right (for finish) end of the predecessor activity, waiting for the cursor to change to a 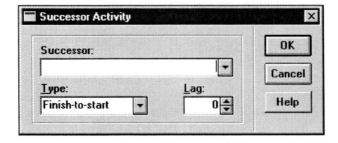 and drag (by holding the left mouse button down) the cursor to the left or right of the successor activity.

If the activity is not visible release the mouse in a blank area and choose the successor using the **Successor Activity** form.

Select the required successor activity from the drop-down box.

To change the relationship or alter the lag of an existing relationship, move the mouse over the relationship line and then left mouse click to display the **Edit Relationships** form.

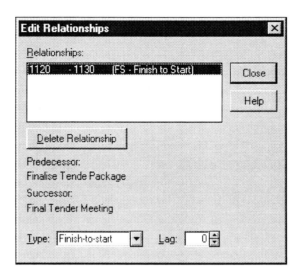

9.3.1 Formatting PERT View Relationships

Select **Format**, **Relationship Lines** to open the **Relationships** form as the first step in tailoring the PERT view.

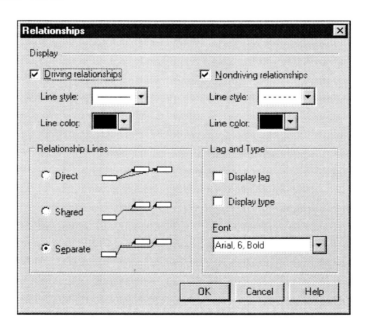

This allows you to choose to:

- Display/not display the driving and Non-driving relationships
- Change the color and line style
- Change to style of drawing the relationship lines
- Display the lag and relationship type in the font of your choice

9.3.2   Formatting PERT Activity Boxes

Select **Format**, **Activity Box Configuration** as the next step in tailoring the PERT view.

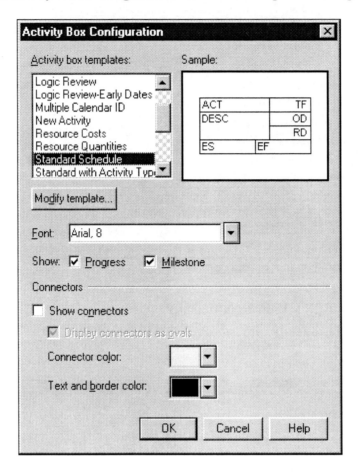

This allows you to:

- Select/modify the contents of each activity box

- Select the font to be used for the text in the box

- Optionally display progress and milestones

- Display/not to display connectors that are not in your current view

- Configure the connectors fill and text/border color

9.3.3 Modify PERT View Activity Box Templates

Modify or create a new template by using the Modify template... icon to display the **Modify Template** form.

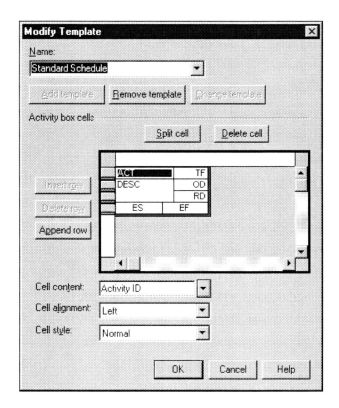

Entering a new template name activates the **Add template** form and allows you to store your modifications under a new name.

Select the cell you wish to modify and then you may:

- Insert a row above the row of that cell

- Delete the row of that cell

- Append a row to the last row of the box

- Split the selected cell in two

- Delete the cell but leave the row and other cells in that row

- Alter the cell contents, alignment or style

9.3.4 Formatting Activity Box Ends and Colors

The next step in tailoring the PERT view is to select **Format, Activity Box Ends and Colors** to open the **Activity Box Ends and Colors** form.

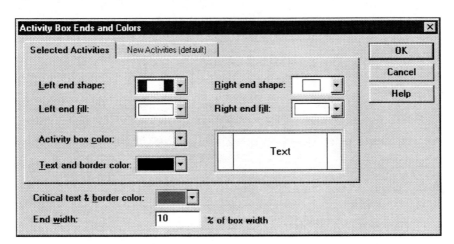

You may tailor the shape, pattern, color and width of the ends of the boxes.

Use a filter or the Shift/Ctrl keys to select multiple activities.

9.3.5   Timescaled PERT

SureTrak Version 3.0 has the facility for displaying a Timescaled PERT diagram which places the activities on a timescale. This option is found under **Format, Organize, Arrangement**.

Non Timescaled PERT Diagram

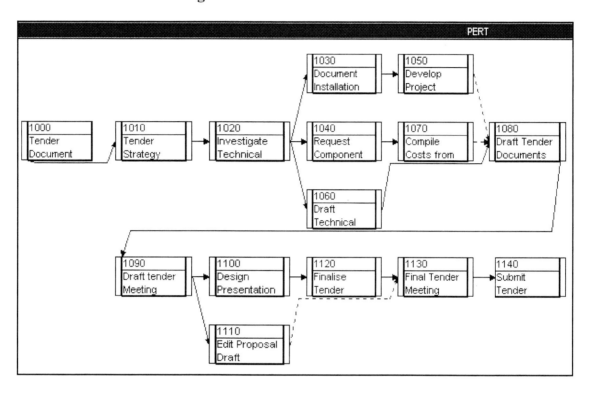

Timescaled PERT Diagram

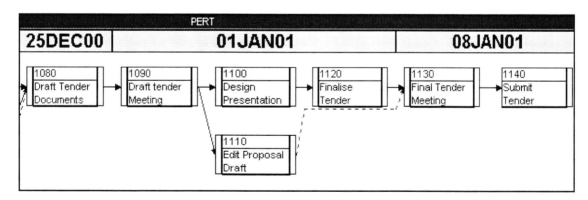

WORKSHOP 10

Adding the Relationships

Preamble

You have determined the logical sequence of activities, so you may now create the relationships.

Assignment

1. Input the logic below using the different methods detailed.

2. Format PERT diagram to reflect the output below.

3. Press F9 to schedule your project.

4. Check your dates, see over for the Bar Chart view.

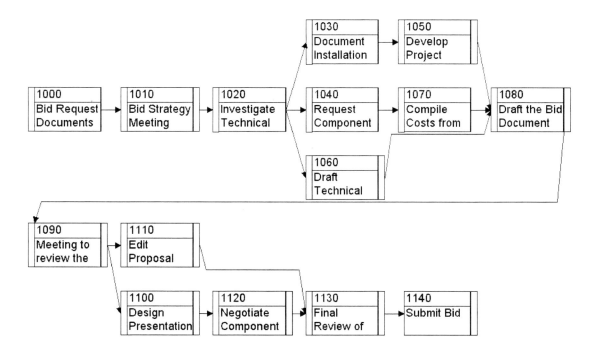

See over page for bar chart view.

Workshop 10 Bar Chart View

Act ID	Description	Orig Dur	Early Start	Early Finish
1000	Bid Request Documents Received	0	01DEC03	
1010	Bid Strategy Meeting	1	01DEC03	01DEC03
1020	Investigate Technical Feasibility	8	02DEC03	11DEC03
1030	Document Installation Requirements	4	12DEC03	16DEC03
1040	Request Component Tenders	3	12DEC03	16DEC03
1050	Develop Project Schedule	4	17DEC03	20DEC03
1060	Draft Technical Details Schedule	9	12DEC03	24DEC03
1070	Compile Costs from Component Bids	2	17DEC03	18DEC03
1080	Draft the Bid Document	3	29DEC03	31DEC03
1090	Meeting to review the Draft Bid	1	02JAN04	02JAN04
1100	Design Presentation	1	05JAN04	05JAN04
1110	Edit Proposal Draft Bid Document	1	05JAN04	05JAN04
1120	Negotiate Component Work Packages	6	06JAN04	13JAN04
1130	Final Review of Bid Document	1	14JAN04	14JAN04
1140	Submit Bid	0		14JAN04

9.4 Scheduling the Project

Now that you have activities and logic in place, it is time to calculate the activity dates. More specifically, you will **Schedule** the project to calculate the Early Dates, Late Dates and the Total Float. This will allow you to determine the **Critical Path** of the project.

To schedule your project, select **Tools**, **Schedule** and check that the **Project data date** is correct.

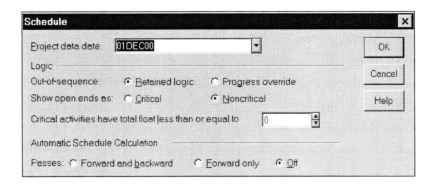

If you know that your data date is correct, then you may simply press **F9** or click on the icon to schedule the project.

When Automatic Schedule calculation is turned off it is possible to edit the Early Dates in the Activity form when the correct option is selected in **Tools**, **Options**, **Defaults** tab. These are then reset when the schedule is recalculated.

To help understand the calculation of late and early dates, float and critical path, we will now manually work through an example. The boxes below represent activities.

ES = Early Start   EF = Early Finish

             DUR = Duration

LS = Late Start   LF = Late Finish

ES	EF
OD	
LS	LF

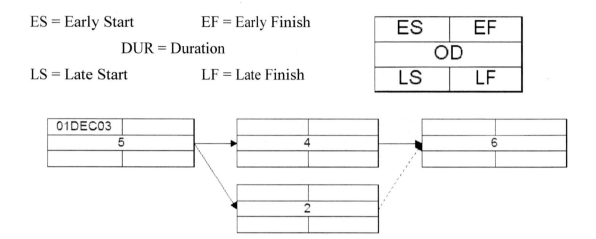

The forward pass calculates the early dates: $EF = ES + DUR - 1$

Start the calculation from the first activity and work forward in time assuming a 7-day working week.

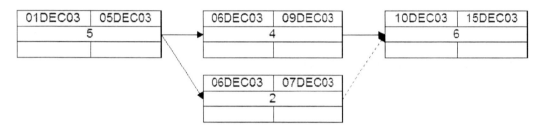

The backward pass calculates the late dates: $LS = LF - DUR + 1$

Start the calculation at the last activity and work backwards in time.

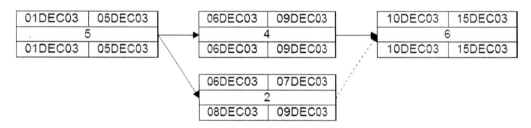

Note: The **Critical Path** is the path where any delay causes a delay in the project.

The solid relationship lines represent **Driving Relationships**, whereas the broken relationship lines represent **Non-driving Relationships**.

Float is the difference between the **Late Finish** minus **Early Finish**. The 2 day duration activity has float of $9 - 7 = 2$. None of the other activities have float.

WORKSHOP 11

Scheduling Calculations

ES	EF
OD	
LS	LF

Assignment

Calculate the early and late dates for the following activities assuming a Monday to Friday working week.

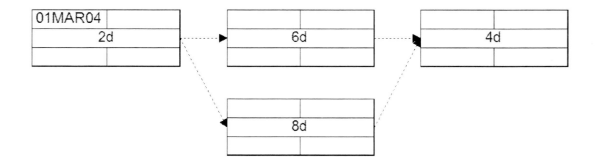

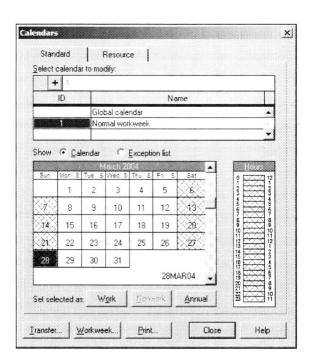

ANSWER

Forward Pass   EF = ES + DUR −1

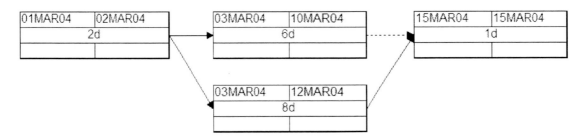

Backward Pass   LS = LF − DUR +1

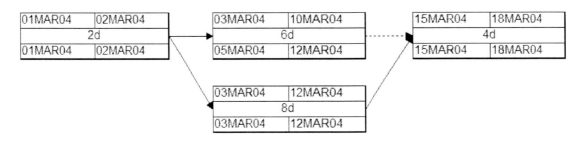

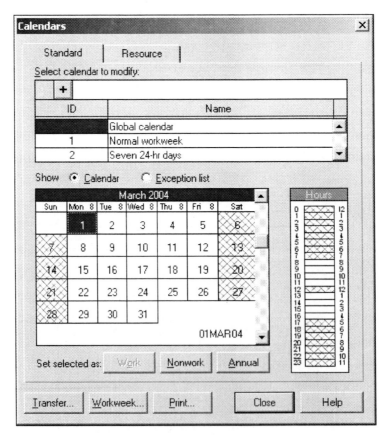

9.5 Constraints

Constraints are used to impose logic on activities that may not be realistically scheduled with logic links. We will deal in detail with four constraints:

- **Start constraint – Early**

- **Finish constraint – Late**

- **Expected Finish**

- **Float constraint – As late as possible**.

These are the minimum number of constraints that required to effectively schedule your project.

Start constraint – Early (also known as "start no earlier than" constraint) is used when the start date of an activity is known or known approximately. SureTrak will not allow the activity's early start prior to this date.

Finish Constraint – Late (also known as "finish no later" constraint) is used when the latest finish date is stipulated. SureTrak will not allow the activity's late finish after this date.

Expected Finish is used to calculate the remaining duration. SureTrak will calculate the remaining duration as the number of working days left between the start date (data date if in progress) and the nominated expected finish.

Float constraint – As late as possible (also known as "zero free float") is used to make the activity early finish immediately prior to its successors. A classical example is the "just in time" delivery of materials before installation.

The other constraints are:

• **Start constraint – Late**	Start no later than
• **Finish constraint – Early**	Finish no earlier than
• **Start on**	Start no earlier than and Start no later than
• **Mandatory Start/Finish**	Nominates the dates and violates the logic
• **Zero total float**	Removes all positive float.

Early Constraints operate on the **Early Dates** and **Late Constraints** operate on **Late Dates**.

9.5.1   Assigning Constraints

To impose constraints on an activity, display the **Constraints** form by either:

- Selecting the activity, pressing the right mouse button, and choosing **Activity Detail**, **Constraints** from the menu

- Using View, Activity Detail and choosing Constraints

- Holding the **Ctrl** key, positioning the mouse over the start or end of a bar and when the cursor turns to a hammer and nail pressing the left mouse button.

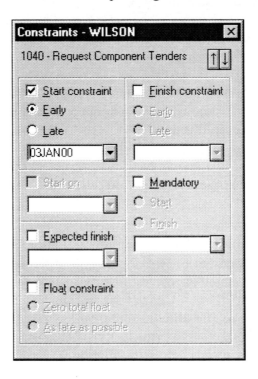

- Click on the Constraint required
- Select the Constraint date required

9.5.2   Project Overview

It is also possible to impose an absolute finish date on the project using the **Project Overview** form.

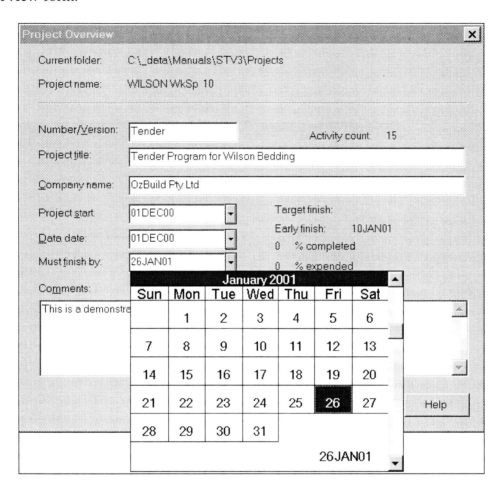

Imposing a **Must finish by** date makes SureTrak calculate the late dates from the **Must finish by** date rather than the calculated early finish date. This will introduce positive float to activities when the calculated **Early finish** date is prior to the **Must finish by** date. This will also create negative float when the activity's calculated early finish date is after to the must finish by date.

 It is not obvious where the float is being generated once a **Must finish by** date is imposed on a project. This is often confusing to people new to scheduling and it is recommended that you do not use a **Must finish by** date. Instead tie all activities to a **Finish milestone** which has a **Late finish** constraint.

9.5.3 Log Records

SureTrak provides ten 48-character log text data items for you to record additional descriptions such as your planning assumptions. Information may be entered into the Log Records by defining Log Texts as columns.

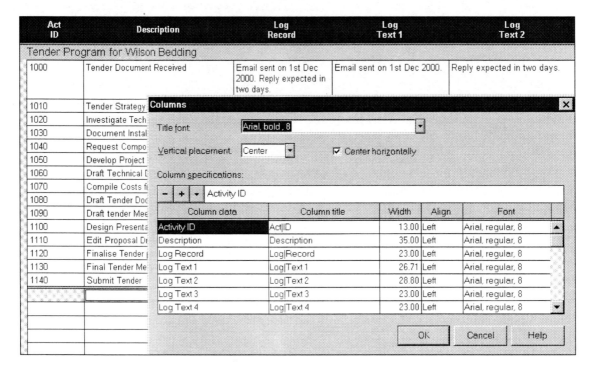

- **Log Text 1** to **Log Text 10** fields may be edited and are used to access the fields individually and

- **Log Record** combines the contents of all ten logs into a single data item that may not be edited.

WORKSHOP 12

Constraints

Preamble
Management has provided further input to your schedule.

Assignment

1. Record the calculated early finish and note the critical path of the project before applying any constraints. Reformat the columns deleting the Activity code columns and display the Total Float column.

2. The client has said that they require the submission on 23JAN04:

    a) Apply a Project Must Finish by constraint of 23JAN04 in the Project Overview form and note the Critical Path and Total Float created by this constraint.

    b) Remove the Project Must Finish by constraint and apply a Finish No Later Than constraint of 23JAN04 to Activity 1140, Submit Bid, and note the change in Critical Path and Total Float.

3. Due to proximity to Christmas, management has requested a delay to the Request Component Bids until first thing in the New Year. Therefore assign an Early Start constraint of 05JAN04 to Activity 1040 and note the impact on the Critical Path and end dates. Consensus decided that a better response and sharper prices will be obtained after the Christmas rush, record this in a log record.

4. In order to see which activities may be shortened, group the activities by Total Float and sort by Remaining Duration (descending).

5. After review, it is agreed that two days can be trimmed from Activity 1120, Negotiate the Component Work Packages, reduce the duration of this activity to 4 days and note the change to the Total Float and Project End Dates.

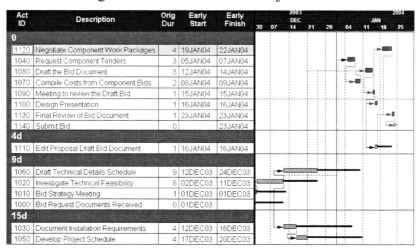

6. Remove Grouping, sort by Activity ID and save your project.

Step 2a

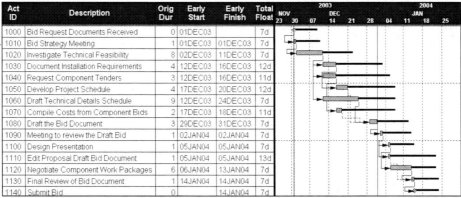

Act ID	Description	Orig Dur	Early Start	Early Finish	Total Float
1000	Bid Request Documents Received	0	01DEC03		7d
1010	Bid Strategy Meeting	1	01DEC03	01DEC03	7d
1020	Investigate Technical Feasibility	8	02DEC03	11DEC03	7d
1030	Document Installation Requirements	4	12DEC03	16DEC03	12d
1040	Request Component Tenders	3	12DEC03	16DEC03	11d
1050	Develop Project Schedule	4	17DEC03	20DEC03	12d
1060	Draft Technical Details Schedule	9	12DEC03	24DEC03	7d
1070	Compile Costs from Component Bids	2	17DEC03	18DEC03	11d
1080	Draft the Bid Document	3	29DEC03	31DEC03	7d
1090	Meeting to review the Draft Bid	1	02JAN04	02JAN04	7d
1100	Design Presentation	1	05JAN04	05JAN04	7d
1110	Edit Proposal Draft Bid Document	1	05JAN04	05JAN04	13d
1120	Negotiate Component Work Packages	6	06JAN04	13JAN04	7d
1130	Final Review of Bid Document	1	14JAN04	14JAN04	7d
1140	Submit Bid	0		14JAN04	7d

Step 2b

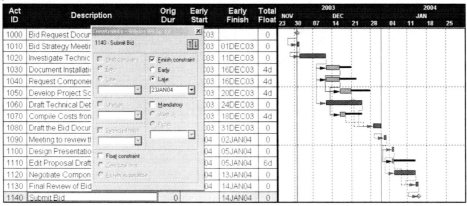

Act ID	Description	Orig Dur	Early Start	Early Finish	Total Float
1000	Bid Request Docur			03	0
1010	Bid Strategy Meetir			03	01DEC03	0
1020	Investigate Technic			03	11DEC03	0
1030	Document Installatio			03	16DEC03	4d
1040	Request Componer			03	16DEC03	4d
1050	Develop Project Sc			03	20DEC03	4d
1060	Draft Technical Det			03	24DEC03	0
1070	Compile Costs fron			03	18DEC03	4d
1080	Draft the Bid Docur			03	31DEC03	0
1090	Meeting to review tl			04	02JAN04	0
1100	Design Presentatio			04	05JAN04	0
1110	Edit Proposal Draft			04	05JAN04	6d
1120	Negotiate Compon			04	13JAN04	0
1130	Final Review of Bid			04	14JAN04	0
1140	Submit Bid	0		14JAN04	0

Step 3

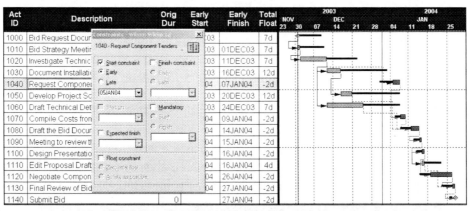

Act ID	Description	Orig Dur	Early Start	Early Finish	Total Float
1000	Bid Request Docur			03		7d
1010	Bid Strategy Meetir			03	01DEC03	7d
1020	Investigate Technic			03	11DEC03	7d
1030	Document Installatio			03	16DEC03	12d
1040	Request Componer			04	07JAN04	-2d
1050	Develop Project Sc			03	20DEC03	12d
1060	Draft Technical Det			03	24DEC03	7d
1070	Compile Costs fron			04	09JAN04	-2d
1080	Draft the Bid Docur			04	14JAN04	-2d
1090	Meeting to review tl			04	15JAN04	-2d
1100	Design Presentatio			04	16JAN04	-2d
1110	Edit Proposal Draft			04	16JAN04	4d
1120	Negotiate Compon			04	26JAN04	-2d
1130	Final Review of Bid			04	27JAN04	-2d
1140	Submit Bid	0		27JAN04	-2d

Step 4

Act ID	Description	Orig Dur	Early Start	Early Finish	Tot Flo
-2d					
1120	Negotiate Component Work Packages	6	19JAN04	26JAN04	-2
1040	Request Component Tenders	3	05JAN04	07JAN04	-2
1080	Draft the Bid Document	3	12JAN04	14JAN04	-2
1070	Compile Costs from Component Bids	2	08JAN04	09JAN04	-2
1090	Meeting to review the Draft Bid	1	15JAN04	15JAN04	-2
1100	Design Presentation	1	16JAN04	16JAN04	-2
1130	Final Review of Bid Document	1	27JAN04	27JAN04	-2
1140	Submit Bid	0		27JAN04	-2
4d					
1110	Edit Proposal Draft Bid Document	1	16JAN04	16JAN04	4
7d					
1060	Draft Technical Details Schedule	9	12DEC03	24DEC03	7
1020	Investigate Technical Feasibility	8	02DEC03	11DEC03	7
1010	Bid Strategy Meeting	1	01DEC03	01DEC03	7
1000	Bid Request Documents Received	0	01DEC03		7
12d					
1030	Document Installation Requirements	4	12DEC03	16DEC03	12
1050	Develop Project Schedule	4	17DEC03	20DEC03	12

10 FILTERS AND LAYOUTS

This chapter covers the ability of SureTrak to control the presentation of information, both on the screen and in printouts by using **Filters** and **Layouts**.

10.1 Understanding Filters

SureTrak has an ability to display only tasks that meet specific criteria. You may wish to only see the Project Manager's work or perhaps Saturday work or even the work over the next couple of months. **SureTrak** defaults to displaying all activities and has a number of filters already available that you might like to use or edit. You can also create one or more of your own.

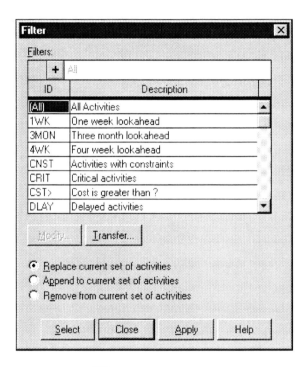

Select **Format, Filter** or click the 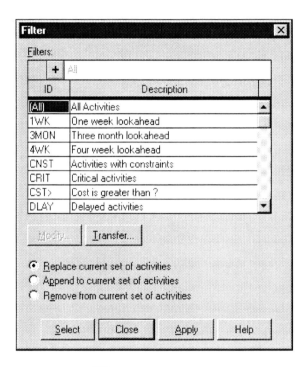 icon on the toolbar to display the **Filter** form:

- **Modify** displays the filter specification for editing the filter criteria.

- **Transfer** is a facility for copying filters from other project files.

- **Replace** only displays activities that meet the filter criteria.

- **Append to** adds activities to the display that meet the filter criteria.

- **Remove from** removes from the display activities that meet the filter criteria.

- **Select** highlights activities that meet the filter's criteria.

- **Apply** applies the selected filter and displays only activities that meet the criteria.

- A filter may also be applied by selecting one from the drop-down box in the **Layout** toolbar.

10.2 Creating and Modifying Filters

We will take you through the process of creating a new filter to display activities that are incomplete.

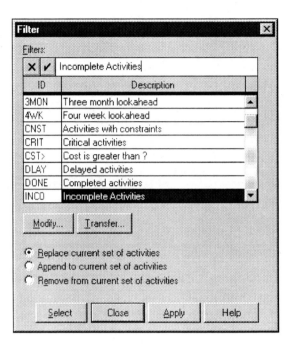

- Press the ⊞ icon or click into a blank line at the bottom of the list of filters to create a new filter.

- Enter the filter **ID**, a maximum of four characters and the filter **Description**, **Incomplete Activities**.

- You also are able to edit the new filter in the **Filter Specification** form.

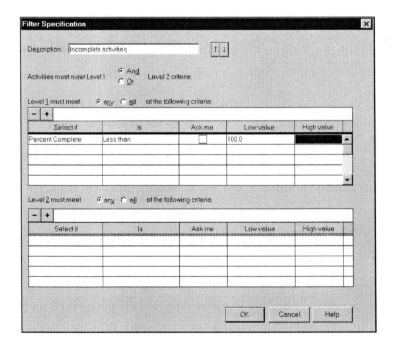

- In the Select if column, select Percent Complete.

- In the **Is** column, select **Less than**.

- Leave **Ask me** blank, this feature will be covered later.

- In the **Low Value** column, type **100**.

- Click [OK] to close the Filter Specification form and [Apply] to apply the filter.

This Incomplete Activity filter demonstrates a simple filter that selects incomplete activities.

More complex filters are possible using Level 1 and Level 2.

Understanding Filter Levels

- **Level 1** and **Level 2** allow you to create some more complex filters that may not be created with only one level.

- The filter and levels have the options of **And** and **Or**.

- At each level you may use up to five criteria for the selection of activities.

- Click [OK] to close the Filter Specification form and [Apply] to apply the filter.

Below is an example of a filter used for showing a four-week look ahead.

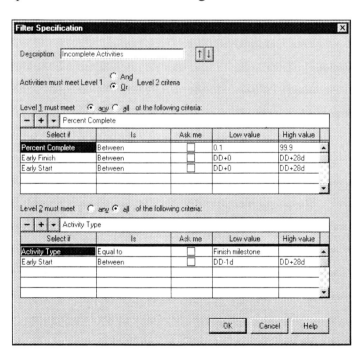

It is suggested that you experiment with the filters to develop an understanding of all that can be achieved with them.

Ask me feature
When you create a filter and tick the **Ask me** box.

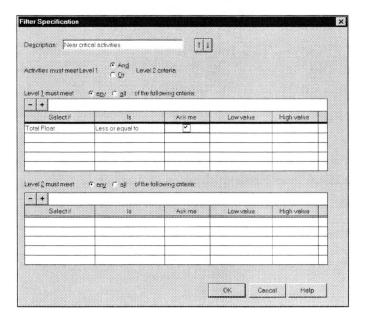

When you apply the filter you will be presented with the **Filter Value** form allowing you to nominate the value required for the filter.

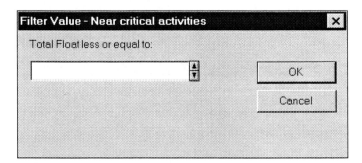

This feature is very useful as now you need only to create one filter which may be used for a number of purposes.

Modifying Filters
Modifying filters follows the same principles as creating filters.

- At the Filter menu select the filter you wish to edit and click on the **Modify** icon.

WORKSHOP 13

Filters

Preamble

Management has asked for reports on activities to suit their requirements.

Assignment

1. Group the activities by Phase, sort by Activity Id (ascending).

2. Add columns for Phase and Responsibility.

3. Create a filter and call it PEP with a description of Estimation and Research. Make it select only the activities from the Estimation phase and the Research phase.

Act ID	Description	Early Start	Early Finish	Phase	Responsibility
Research					
1000	Bid Request Documents Received	01DEC03		R	CFP
1010	Bid Strategy Meeting	01DEC03	01DEC03	R	DTW
1020	Investigate Technical Feasibility	02DEC03	11DEC03	R	SSM
Estimate					
1030	Document Installation Requirements	12DEC03	16DEC03	E	SSM
1040	Request Component Tenders	05JAN04	07JAN04	E	ARL
1070	Compile Costs from Component Bids	08JAN04	09JAN04	E	ARL

4. Run this filter noting the activities selected and their Responsibility codes.

5. Now add additional criteria to select only those activities for which Scott Morrison or Angela Lowe are responsible.

6. Run this filter and note the difference.

Act ID	Description	Early Start	Early Finish	Phase	Responsibility
Research					
1020	Investigate Technical Feasibility	02DEC03	11DEC03	R	SSM
Estimate					
1030	Document Installation Requirements	12DEC03	16DEC03	E	SSM
1040	Request Component Tenders	05JAN04	07JAN04	E	ARL
1070	Compile Costs from Component Bids	08JAN04	09JAN04	E	ARL

10.3 Layouts

Rather than restricting the data with filters, **Layouts** alter the presentation. The formatting undertaken so far has altered the default **Layout**. You may create as many layouts as you like, save them and then you may switch between the layouts as you require.

Layouts are not stored as part of the project file but are common to all projects and each layout is a file located in the sub-directory nominated in **Tools, Options, Directories**.

Select **View, Layouts** to apply the layout you desire or as with the filters you may create one that suits your needs. The 🖼 icon on the toolbar will also access the layouts.

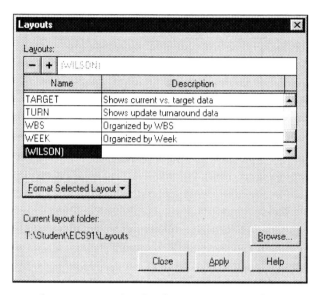

- Select ⊞ to create a layout, type in the layout **Name** of up to eight characters and enter the **Description**. When an existing layout is selected before creating a new layout, the new layout is a clone of the existing one as all settings are the same.

- Select ⊟ to delete a layout.

- **Apply** applies a selected layout to the display. You may also use the drop-down box in the **Layout** toolbar to select and apply a layout.

- **Format Selected Layout** edits the following format characteristics of each layout:
  ➤ Columns
  ➤ Row Height
  ➤ Organize
  ➤ Bars
  ➤ Relationship Lines
  ➤ Timescale/Sight Lines
  ➤ Resource Profile/Table
  ➤ Summary Bars
  ➤ Summarize All and Screen Colors

- Browse Allows you to change the Current Layout Folder.

WORKSHOP 14

Layouts

Preamble

We need a new report Layout that we will print when required.

Assignment

1. Apply the All Activities filter.
2. Create a new layout WS14 titled Workshop 14 with the following settings:

   Columns
   > Activity ID, Arial 8, Centre Aligned
   > Description, Arial 8, Left Aligned
   > Original Duration, Arial 8, Centre Aligned
   > Early Start, Arial 8, Arial 8, Centre Aligned
   > Late Finish, Arial 8 Bold, Centre Aligned

   Bars
   > Early Bar
   > – Place Description Arial 6, above the bar
   > – Remove Start and Finish points
   > Float Bar
   > – Make the bar size 1 in position 1
   > – Display a Total Float point (Late Finish Point) in position 1

   Organized
   > Group by
   > – Department (font Arial, bold, 10) and then
   > – Phase (font Arial, bold, 10)
   > Sort on Early Start

   Timescale
   > Weeks

3. Check your answer with the picture over the page and your project.

Your view should look like this:

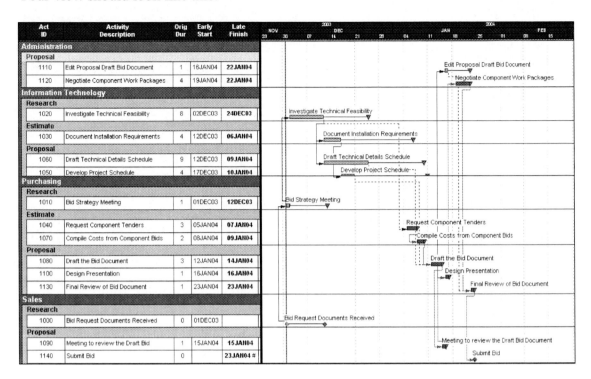

11 PRINTING AND REPORTS

You are now at the stage to print the schedule so other people may review and comment on it. This chapter will examine of the many of the options for printing your project.

Print settings apply to all **Layouts** and are not saved as part of a layout.

11.1 Printing the Bar Chart

Select **File**, **Print Preview** or use the icon on the toolbar to view the printout in the print preview view

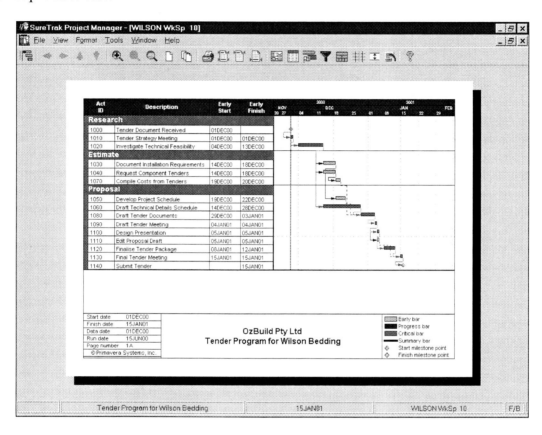

From left to right the following describes the functions of the icons at the top of the screen:

- The icon on the left returns you to the normal view

- The arrows allow scrolling when a printout has more than one page

- The magnifying glass zooms in and zooms out

- The next two icons display one or all pages

- The next four are for **Printing**, **Page set-up**, **Header** and **Footer set-up**

- The next group accesses the **Layout** and **Formatting** settings

- The last is **Help**.

11.2 Page Setup

Click the 📇 icon on the toolbar or select **File**, **Page Setup** to display the **Page Setup** form.

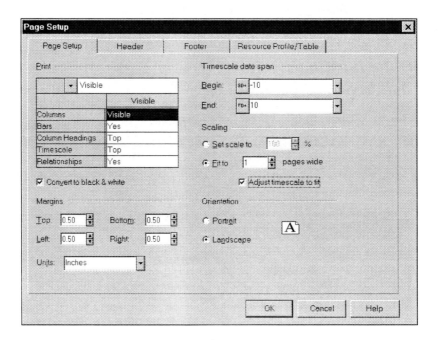

The **Page Setup** form contains the following tabs:

- Page Setup
- Header
- Footer
- Resource Profile/Table

11.2.1 Page Setup Tab

In the **Page Setup** tab:

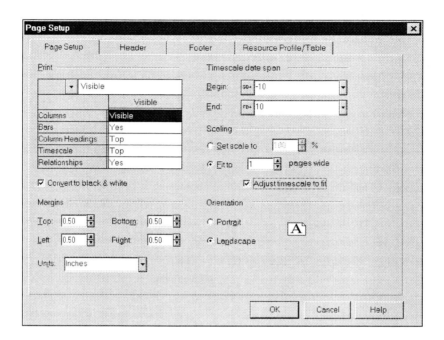

- Click on the top left hand box below print to select to print **All, Visible** or **None** of the columns that are displayed in the normal view.

- The drop-down boxes next to **Columns, Bars, Column Headings, Time Scale** and **Relationships** allow you to select what you wish to display in the print out.

- **Convert to black & white** is useful for faxing print outs, as grey scales are not printed.

- **Begin** and **End** specify the time scale of the bar chart to be printed. These dates are set in the same way as the **Timescale** is formatted.

- **Scaling, Margins** and **Orientation** allow you to specify how the printout will fit on the page.

Adjust the **Fix to pages wide** to 1 otherwise the printout becomes as wide as it needs to be by "tiling" the pages horizontally. This can cause it to look like a jigsaw puzzle.

When you select **Adjust timescale to fit** the font will be printed at the specified size and the timescale will be adjusted to fit the remaining page. This is often the best presentation setting.

 The date range set in **Page Setup** is totally independent from the data range you set in the **Format Timescale** form.

11.2.2 Headers and Footers Tabs

Headers appear at the top of the screen and footers at the bottom, and are both formatted in the same way.

We will discuss the setting of footers.

Click on the **Footer** tab from the **Page Setup** tab or select from the print preview icons. This may display the default footers and headers, but you should modify the output to suit your requirements.

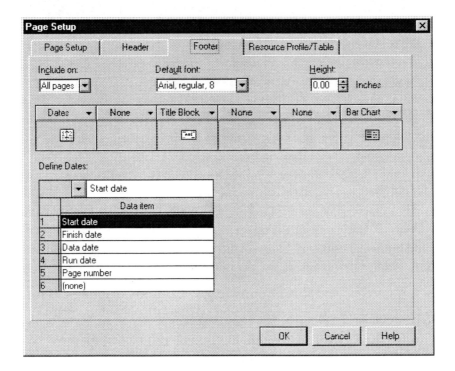

- **Include on** allows you to select which pages the header of footer is printed on – **All**, **First**, **Last** or **None**.

- **Default font** specifies the font for all the text, but the title block may have a different font by clicking on the **Font** icon when selecting the **Title Block**.

- **Height** is used to specify the height of the headers and footers if they become distorted.

Use the drop-down menu above the left box to select the **Dates** field. You may insert the data items as shown above.

Use the drop-down menu third from the left to select **Title Block**, completing it as shown. You may select data from the drop-down boxes on the **Left**, **Centre** or **Right**.

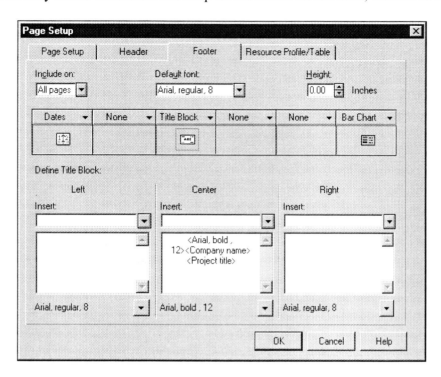

Next highlight the text and change the font of the title block.

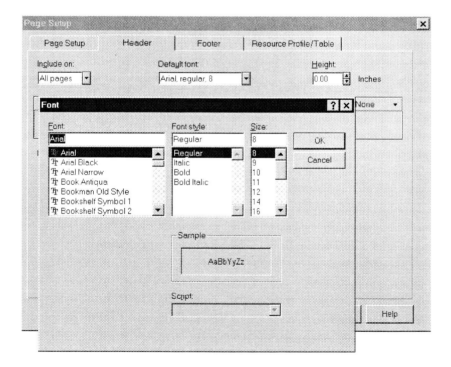

Now, use the drop-down menu on the right hand side to select **Revision Box**, completing it as shown.

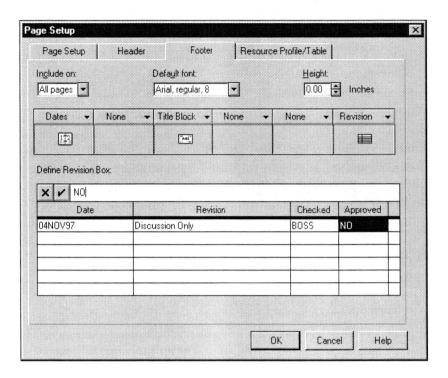

- **Height** sets the maximum height of the header and footer.

Find your way back out to the print preview screen by clicking **OK**, and then click **File**, **Print** or click the 🖨 icon on the toolbar to print your report.

If you select the **Bar Chart Legend** but do not wish to see all the bars then you may hide the bars displayed in the legend by selecting **Format**, **Bars**, **Options** and check the bars you do not wish to see as **No** in the **Visible** column.

 Each time you report to the client or management we recommended taking a complete copy of your project. This allows you to reproduce these reports at any time in the future. You may save the project into the same directory provided you change the file name.

WORKSHOP 15

Reports

Preamble

After we issued our WS14 – Workshop 14 report we received a request to tailor it further.

Assignment

1. Modify this layout to have:

    – Titles – add the word "Draft" to appear under the Project title and Company name.

    – Dates – Remove the page number from the dates.

    – Revision Box – replace the legend with a revision box.

    – Logo – place any logo next to the revision box.

2. Check your results with the picture over the page.

3. Save your project.

4. Save your project as WILSON01, which will be used in a later Workshop.

5. Close WILSON01 and reopen WILSON.

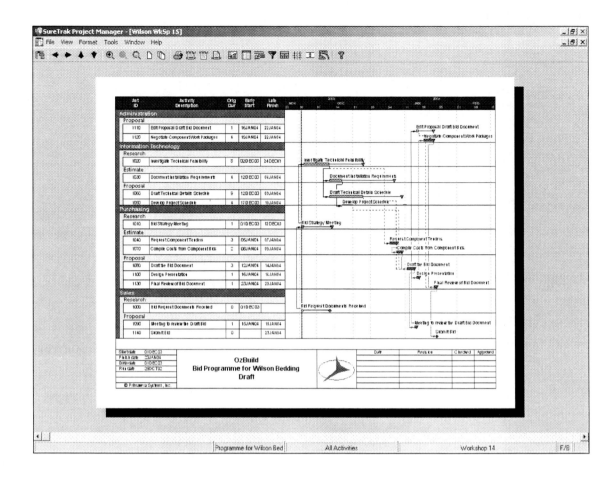

11.3 Reports

All print settings including headers and footers set in the previous section will apply to all layouts.

Reports allow you to define alternative print settings that are saved with each report.

You should use reports when you require:

- Unique **Footers** and **Headers** for a print out

- To print more than one printout at a time.

Select **Tools**, **Reports** to open the **Reports** form where you may create, modify and delete reports.

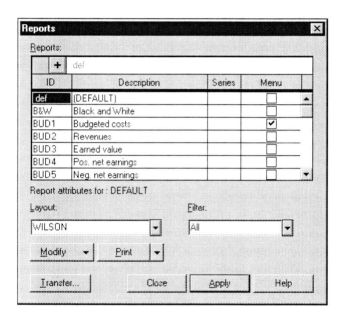

Once again, you can see that there are several reports already set up which you can use or modify to suit your own requirements.

When you create a **Report** select a **Layout** and a **Filter** to be associated with the report. Unique **Footers** and **Headers** and other printing settings may be saved with the report.

Select **Tools, Options, View** tab to nominate if a report is to be printed or applied to a view when the report is **Applied** by clicking the ⎣ **Apply** ⎦ button in the **Reports** form.

Note: This chapter is not intended to cover reports in detail, but to make you aware of them so that you can investigate reports further on your own.

11.4 Manual Page Breaks

SureTrak automatically calculates page breaks to suit the page size and margins you nominate in page set-up. You may also manually place page breaks at any activity or banding in the schedule.

Before you insert a page break it is suggested that you display the page breaks by selecting **View**, **Page Breaks**. This will place a grey strip down the left-hand side of the screen.

- Page breaks are calculated automatically by SureTrak and are indicated by an indented arrow ▨ on the grey strip and

- Manually placed breaks appear as raised arrows ▧ on the grey strip.

To insert, remove and manipulate manually placed page breaks:

- Highlight the line above which you require the page break and select **Insert**, **Page Break** to insert the break. Other automatically placed pages breaks will be recalculated.

- Page breaks may also be added by clicking in the grey strip on the left-hand side of the screen.

- Page breaks may be moved by clicking on an arrow of an existing manually placed page break in the grey strip and dragging it up or down.

- To remove a manually inserted page break, highlight the line and select **Insert**, **Delete Page Break** or click on the break in the grey strip and drag to the right when a cross appears.

- Select **Insert**, **Clear All Page Breaks** to remove all manually placed page breaks.

- **View**, **Repaginate** or click on the ▣ icon above the grey strip to recalculate the page breaks after you have made formatting changes such as changing the row height or changing the sort order.

12 TRACKING PROGRESS

You have completed the plan or have completed sufficient iterations to have an acceptable plan, and the project is progressing. Now the important phase of regular monitoring begins. Monitoring is important to help catch problems as early as possible, and thus to help minimize the impact of the problem on the successful completion of the project.

The main steps for monitoring progress are:

- Setting the **Target dates** – these are the dates against which progress is compared

- Record or mark-up progress

- Update or status the schedule

- Compare and report actual progress against planned progress and revise the schedule if required.

Often a statusing report, such as the one below, is printed out with page breaks at each responsible person. This report is distributed for them to mark up the projects progress and returned it to the scheduler. It has a filter applied that displays the activities that are incomplete and those that will start in the next few weeks.

Act ID	Activity Description	% Comp	Revised %	Planned Duration	Rem Dur	Revised Rem Dur	Early Start	Actual or Exptd Start	Early Finish	Actual or Exptd Finish	Suspend Date	Resume Date
Angela Lowe - Purchasing												
1040	Request Component Tenders	0		3	3		14DEC00		18DEC00			
1070	Compile Costs from Tenders	0		2	2		19DEC00		20DEC00			
Carol Peterson - Tender Manager												
1000	Tender Document Received	0		0	0		01DEC00					
David Williams - Accounts Manager												
1010	Tender Strategy Meeting	0		1	1		01DEC00		01DEC00			
1080	Draft Tender Documents	0		3	3		29DEC00		03JAN01			
Scott Morrison - Systems Analyst												
1020	Investigate Technical Feasibility	0		8	8		04DEC00		13DEC00			
1030	Document Installation	0		4	4		14DEC00		18DEC00			
1050	Develop Project Schedule	0		4	4		19DEC00		22DEC00			
1060	Draft Technical Details Schedule	0		9	9		14DEC00		28DEC00			

12.1 Setting the Target

Setting the Target copies the planned start and planned finish dates into fields titled **Target Start** and **Target Finish**. Once you have set the Target dates you will be able to compare your progress with your original plan. You will be able to see if you are ahead or behind schedule and by how much. If you do not set the Target dates you will be unable to compare your progress with your original plan. Setting the Target dates should be completed before you status the schedule for the first time.

Select **Define**, **Target Dates** to display the **Targets** form.

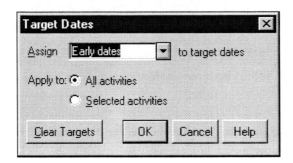

- **Assign** allows selection of the **Early Dates**, **Late Dates** or **Unleveled Dates** to be copied into the Target dates fields.

- You may set or reset the Target of some activities by highlighting them and clicking on **Selected Activities** in the **Target Dates** form.

- **Clear** removes the Target dates from the Target dates fields.

- You may also display the Target date columns and edit them directly.

The form above shows the default settings which selects **All Activities** and the **Early dates**. This is the normal method of setting the baseline. Now you can input the mark-up without fear of losing the original dates. This also will enable you to compare the progress with the original plan.

Setting the Target dates does not store the logic or constraints.

The Target dates column may be displayed and the dates edited.

Target dates may not be set when the project has been saved as Concentric (P3) as they are nominated in P3 (see section 3.1).

12.2 Recording Progress

Normally a project has a nominated status date that could be typically once a week or once a month. Progress is recorded on the status date and the scheduler updates the schedule upon receipt of the information.

The **Remaining Duration** is the period of time from the **Data Date** to the **Early Finish** of the activity. When a project is marked up, it is best to concentrate on the remaining duration of any activity and not the percentage complete. This is because the durations begin as estimates and, as the project progresses, you should get a better idea of how long the task will take to complete.

Typical information recorded for each activity when statusing a project is:

- The activity start date

- The number of days the **activity** still has to go

- The percentage complete and

- If complete, the activity finish date.

A mark-up is often done in pen on a copy of the current schedule and ideally should be prepared by a physical inspection of the work, although that is not always possible. It is good practice to keep this record for your own reference at later date. Ensure that you note the date of the mark-up (ie the data date) and, if relevant the time.

A mark-up sheet would often have a filter displaying only activities that are in progress or will start in the next two periods, and should have sufficient space for people to write in information on the printout.

SureTrak also has an e-mail facility that may be used for gathering status information. This is not covered in this manual.

12.3 Spotlight and Highlighting Activities for Statusing

SureTrak has a facility for highlighting the activities that should have progressed in the status period. The Spotlight facility moves a curtain in the bar chart and highlights the activities that should have progressed or you may simply drag the data date to create the curtain.

12.3.1 Spotlighting Activities Using Spotlight Icon

The Spotlight facility highlights all activities that should have progressed. Click on the ⬛ toolbar icon and the curtain will move forward in time in the smallest displayed unit on time scale. The ⬛ icon may be clicked a number of times until the required date is reached.

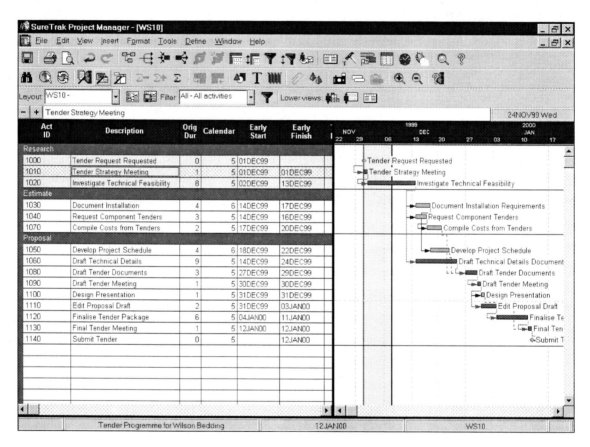

Press the **Shift** key and ⬛ icon to decrease the number of time periods.

12.3.2 Highlighting Activities for Updating by Dragging the Data Date

To highlight activities for updating, hold the mouse arrow on the Data Date line, display the double-headed arrow ⟷, press the left mouse button and drag the data date line to the required date. All the activities that should have been worked in the time period are highlighted.

12.4 Update the schedule

The next stage is to update the schedule by entering the mark-up information into SureTrak.

SureTrak provides several methods of statusing the schedule:

- **Update Progress** is an automated process that assumes all activities have progressed as planned

- **Update Activity** statuses activities one at a time or

- the Activity form

Before we cover these methods it is important to understand the facility to **Link remaining duration and schedule percent complete**.

12.4.1 Link Remaining Duration and Schedule Percent Complete

If you select in **Options**, **Resource** to **Link remaining duration and schedule percent complete** then Remaining Duration and % Complete will change proportionally.

This means that you are unable to enter the percentage complete independently from the Remaining Duration. As the Remaining Duration decreases the Percent Complete will increase.

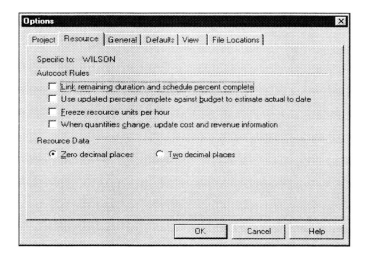

It is suggested that you unlink Remaining Duration and Percentage Complete so that you may enter any value for the Remaining Duration and Percent Complete. If you are in a situation where you are not able to calculate a Percent Complete then they may remain linked and SureTrak will calculate a percent complete based on the Remaining Duration.

12.4.2 Statusing Using Update Progress

To update a schedule using the **Update Progress** form select **Tools, Update Progress**.

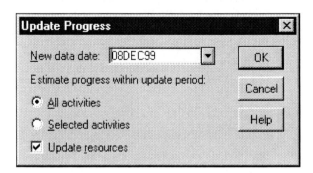

- There are two options for setting the **New data date**:

- You may use the highlight facility before opening the **Update Progress** form and the **New data date** will be set to the highlighted Data Date; or

- You may select the **New data date** when opening the form.

- Decide if you want to status **All activities** or **Selected activities**. To status selected activities highlight the activities (hold the **Ctrl** key and click on the ones you wish to status) before selecting **Tools, Update Progress**.

- Select **Update Resources** if you wish to status the resources. Resource statusing covered in the chapter **STATUSING PROJECTS WITH RESOURCES**.

- Click on **OK** and the schedule will be statused as if all activities were completed according to schedule.

It is often useful to status a project using **Update Progress** before completing the status manually, especially when there are not many changes to the schedule.

 P3 and SureTrak users may use **Update Progress** as a method of reversing the status of activities without having to uncheck the actual start and actual finish of all activities.

12.4.3 Statusing Using Update Activity, Suspend and Resume

To input the mark-up information, firstly highlight the activities that should have been worked using the Spotlight facility.

Now click on the first activity and use the right mouse button display the menu and click on **Update Activity** or select **Tools, Update Activity**.

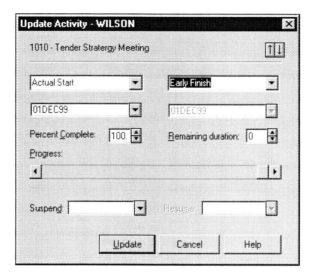

- Select **Actual Start** from the Drop-down menu and select the start date if the activity has started.

- Nominate the **% Complete** and **Remaining Duration** or slide the **Progress** bar to adjust the **% Complete**.

- Use **Suspend** and **Resume** if the activity has a break in it and nominate the Activity **Suspend** and **Resume** dates.

- Select **Actual Finish** and select the finish date completed activities.

- **Suspend** and **Resume** facility allows a break in any progress activity that has started. The **Suspend** date is in the past and the **Resume** date is in the future.

- Use the **up** and **down** arrows to scroll through activities to update.

- Once all necessary activities have been updated, select **Update** to accept all updates and exit.

Alternatively, you can enter the relevant data and move on to the next activity, leaving the **Update Activity** form open as you go. Normally the project will not have gone according to plan. Some activities that were supposed to be finished will be while other activities will have started ahead of or behind schedule.

12.4.4 Statusing Using Activity Form

The activity form may also be used for statusing activities in a similar way to the **Update Activity** form.

Before Activity has Started

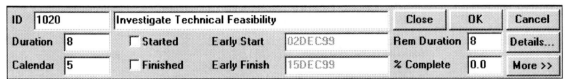

- Click on the **Started** box and select the **Actual Start** date from the **Actual Start** drop-down box

- Set the **Rem(aining) Duration** and **% Complete** if the activity is in progress

In progress Activity

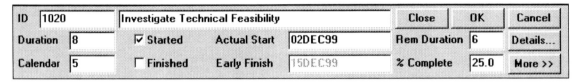

- Click the **Finished** box if the activity is complete and select the **Actual Finish** from the **Actual Finish** drop-down box

Completed Activity

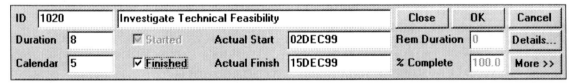

- Should you wish to Suspend or Resume an activity then you will have to open the **Update Activity** form.

WORKSHOP 16

Updating Progress

Preamble

You are at the end of the first week and need to update the progress and reforecast your project.

Assignment

1. Reorganize your layout as below, sorted by Activity ID.

2. Store the Target dates for comparison.

3. Format the Early Bar to show progress as percent complete.

4. Ensure that the **Percentage Complete** and **Remaining Duration** are unlinked.

5. Use Update Progress to re-schedule as at 8DEC03. When the Timescale is set to Weeks you may use the Progress Spotlight icon ⊡ to move the data date forward one week.

6. Status the project using the data from below.

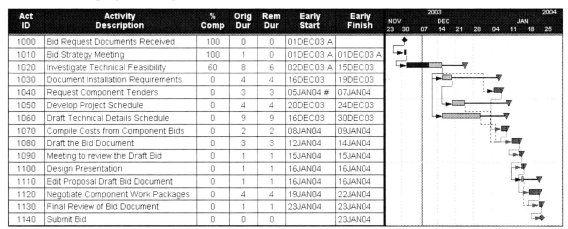

Act ID	Activity Description	% Comp	Orig Dur	Rem Dur	Early Start	Early Finish
1000	Bid Request Documents Received	100	0	0	01DEC03 A	
1010	Bid Strategy Meeting	100	1	0	01DEC03 A	01DEC03 A
1020	Investigate Technical Feasibility	60	8	6	02DEC03 A	15DEC03
1030	Document Installation Requirements	0	4	4	16DEC03	19DEC03
1040	Request Component Tenders	0	3	3	05JAN04 #	07JAN04
1050	Develop Project Schedule	0	4	4	20DEC03	24DEC03
1060	Draft Technical Details Schedule	0	9	9	16DEC03	30DEC03
1070	Compile Costs from Component Bids	0	2	2	08JAN04	09JAN04
1080	Draft the Bid Document	0	3	3	12JAN04	14JAN04
1090	Meeting to review the Draft Bid	0	1	1	15JAN04	15JAN04
1100	Design Presentation	0	1	1	16JAN04	16JAN04
1110	Edit Proposal Draft Bid Document	0	1	1	16JAN04	16JAN04
1120	Negotiate Component Work Packages	0	4	4	19JAN04	22JAN04
1130	Final Review of Bid Document	0	1	1	23JAN04	23JAN04
1140	Submit Bid	0	0	0		23JAN04

7. Save you layout as WS16 titled Status Layout, do not save any changes to the WS14 layout.

8. Save your project.

12.5 Comparison

There will have been some changes to the schedule. The full extent of the change is not apparent without having a Target to compare with. To display the **Target Bar** in the **Bar Chart** select **Format**, **Bars**, scroll down and make the **Target Bar** visible.

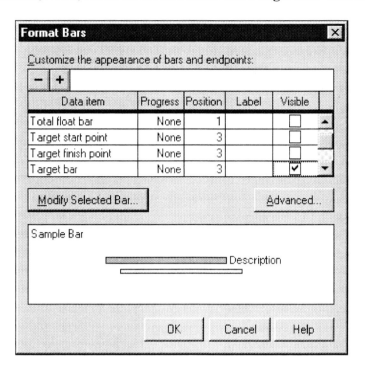

Click **OK** to view the results (slippage of up to two days is displayed below).

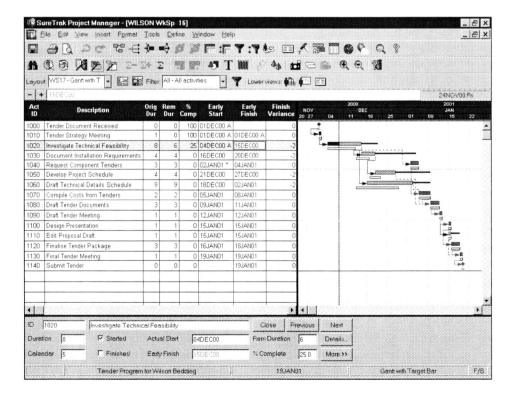

12.6 Corrective Action

There are two courses of action available with slippage. The first is to accept the slippage. This is rarely acceptable, but it is the easy answer. Secondly, and in reality, you should now look to see if you can improve the new end date.

Solutions to return the project to its original completion date must be cleared with the person responsible for the project, as they obviously impact on the work.

Suggested solutions to bring the project back on track include:

- Reducing the durations of activities on or near the critical path. When activities are resourced this may include increasing the number of resources working on the activity.

- Changing activity relationships so activities take place concurrently. This may be achieved by adding a negative lag to a finish to start relationship.

- Changing calendars, say from a five-day to six-day calendar, so activities are being work on for more days per week.

- Reducing the project scope and deleting activities.

WORKSHOP 17

Baseline Comparison

Preamble

At the end of the first week you have updated the schedule and now need to report progress and slippage.

Assignment

1. Format to show Early Bar and Target Bar as well as columns to reflect the layout below. You will observe some activity end dates have been delayed by 2 days.

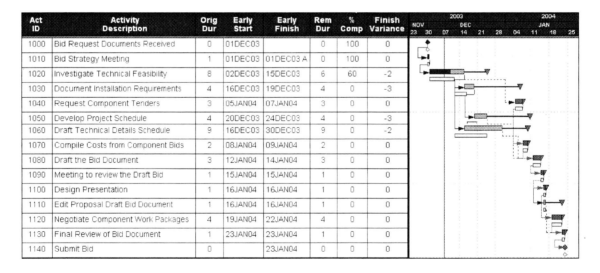

Act ID	Activity Description	Orig Dur	Early Start	Early Finish	Rem Dur	% Comp	Finish Variance
1000	Bid Request Documents Received	0	01DEC03		0	100	0
1010	Bid Strategy Meeting	1	01DEC03	01DEC03 A	0	100	0
1020	Investigate Technical Feasibility	8	02DEC03	15DEC03	6	60	-2
1030	Document Installation Requirements	4	16DEC03	19DEC03	4	0	-3
1040	Request Component Tenders	3	05JAN04	07JAN04	3	0	0
1050	Develop Project Schedule	4	20DEC03	24DEC03	4	0	-3
1060	Draft Technical Details Schedule	9	16DEC03	30DEC03	9	0	-2
1070	Compile Costs from Component Bids	2	08JAN04	09JAN04	2	0	0
1080	Draft the Bid Document	3	12JAN04	14JAN04	3	0	0
1090	Meeting to review the Draft Bid	1	15JAN04	15JAN04	1	0	0
1100	Design Presentation	1	16JAN04	16JAN04	1	0	0
1110	Edit Proposal Draft Bid Document	1	16JAN04	16JAN04	1	0	0
1120	Negotiate Component Work Packages	4	19JAN04	22JAN04	4	0	0
1130	Final Review of Bid Document	1	23JAN04	23JAN04	1	0	0
1140	Submit Bid	0		23JAN04	0	0	0

2. Save you layout as WS17 titled Target Bar and Variance.

13 ORGANIZING ACTIVITIES – ACTIVITY ID CODES, WBS CODES AND OUTLINING

Activity Codes were discussed earlier as a method of organizing activities under project breakdown structures. There are three alternative tools available in SureTrak for organizing activities in a schedule:

- Activity ID Codes

- WBS Codes

- Outlining

13.1 Activity ID Codes

The Activity ID Code is assigned as part of the Activity ID. These codes are different to the previously covered Activity Codes.

Activities assigned with Activity ID Codes are organized in **Layouts** using the same method as activities assigned with Activity Codes. You have the option of choosing **Activity Codes** or **Activity IDs** when creating a Layout.

In the example below, an Activity ID Code has been assigned as the Subproject and the value is seen in the first two characters in the Activity ID.

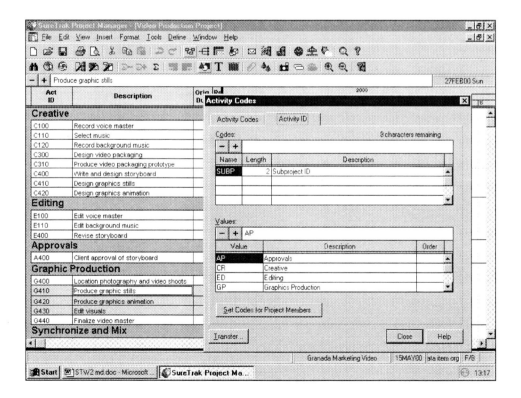

13.1.1 Defining Activity IDs

Select **Define**, **Activity Codes** and the **Activity ID** tab in the **Activity Codes** form.

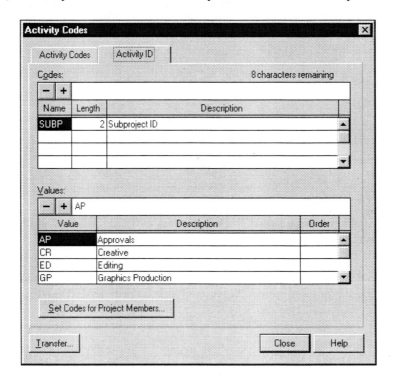

- Use ⊡ or click in the first blank line to create and name a new Activity ID Code.

- **Length** will indicate the maximum number of characters the Activity ID the code may use.

- **Value** and **Order** are entered in the same way as Activity Codes.

- The **Value** is typed in as part of the Activity ID.

- **Transfer** allows importing of codes from another project.

When more than one Activity ID Code dictionary is created then the first dictionary defines the first characters in the Activity ID, the second Activity ID Code defining the next characters and so on.

Activity ID Codes are selected and used in **Layouts** in the same ways as Activity Codes. Activity Codes and Activity ID Codes may be mixed in the same layout.

You are restricted to 10 characters in an Activity ID, therefore it is recommended that you keep the code length of Activity IDs as short as possible to allow some characters for defining unique Activity IDs.

13.1.2 Disadvantage of Activity ID Codes

Complex use of Activity ID Codes may make it difficult to add new activities. You will have to type in the correct codes in the Act ID when adding an activity.

13.1.3 Advantages of Activity ID Codes

Well planned Activity IDs make it easy to find activities and to add logic in large projects. When you type the first characters representing the Activity ID in an Activity ID drop-down box the software takes you to the correct place in the list of activities.

It is suggested that you consider using:

- **Activity ID Codes** for activity attributes that are unlikely to change such as Phase or Discipline and use.

- **Activity Codes** for attributes that may change, such as Responsibility or Contractor.

13.2 WBS – Work Breakdown Structure

A WBS represents a hierarchical breakdown of a project into elements. A WBS may be used to represent any of the following:

- WBS **Work Breakdown Structure**, breaking down the project into the Work required to complete a project;

- OBS **Organization Breakdown Structure**, showing the hierarchical structure of a project;

- CBS **Contract Breakdown Structure**, showing the breakdown of contracts;

- SBS **System Breakdown Structure**, showing the elements of a complex system.

SureTrak allows one hierarchical WBS structure and, therefore, only one of the above structures may be defined with WBS.

It is recommended that you use Activity Codes for Project Breakdown Structures unless you have specific requirements for a hierarchical WBS.

The SureTrak Work Breakdown Structure is a hierarchical structure to which activities are assigned.

- Costs, durations and logic may not be applied to WBS codes; they are purely a structure to attach activities.

- Costs, resources and durations may be summarized at WBS levels.

- A maximum of 20 levels are available.

13.2.1 Creating a WBS Structure

To use the WBS facility the following steps should be followed:

- Set up the WBS levels

- Build the WBS code dictionary

- Assign the code to activities

13.2.2 Set up the WBS Levels

Select **Define**, **WBS Codes**, **Modify Structure** to display the **WBS Structure** form.

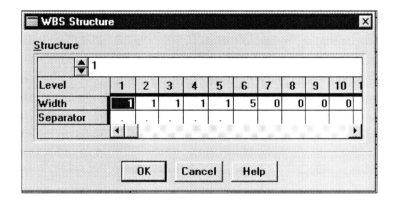

- **Width** is the number of characters you nominate per WBS level.

- **Separator** is the character that is displayed between the level codes.

- Select **OK**.

 Be careful if you wish to redefine the code width after defining and assigning WBS codes. It is likely that the code will end up meaningless and some WBS codes may be deleted.

13.2.3 Building the WBS Code Dictionary

You will now be returned to the **WBS Codes** form.

- The code is typed in the WBS column. Do not type in the separators.

- The title is typed in the **Title** column.

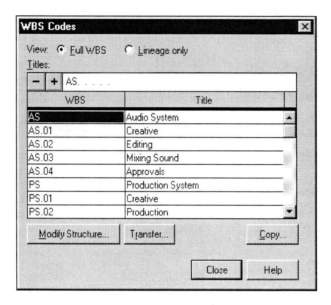

- **Full WBS** is for selecting all WBS Levels after selecting Lineage.

- **Lineage only** filters out one branch of a WBS code for analyzing.

- **Transfer** allows the copying of a WBS from another project.

- **Copy** is used to copy and rename a branch of a WBS.

13.2.4 Assign the Code to Activities

WBS codes are assigned to activities by either:

- Using the WBS code box in the **Task** form

- Displaying the WBS column

- Dragging activities into the correct area when the project is organized by a WBS Layout

13.2.5 Organizing By WBS

To organize by WBS select the WBS radio button when creating a layout using organize.

13.3 Outlining

You will understand **Outlining** if you are familiar with Microsoft Project. Outlining is the main method of organizing activities in Microsoft Project.

Outlining is similar to a WBS but the parent activities are the hierarchical WBS. This is where activities may be promoted and made Summary Activities of lower level activities. The promoted activities are called **Topic Activities**.

The example below shows two levels of outline. **Outline Code 1** is a **Topic** Activity and has its total duration made up of the durations of **Outline Code 1.1** to **1.3**.

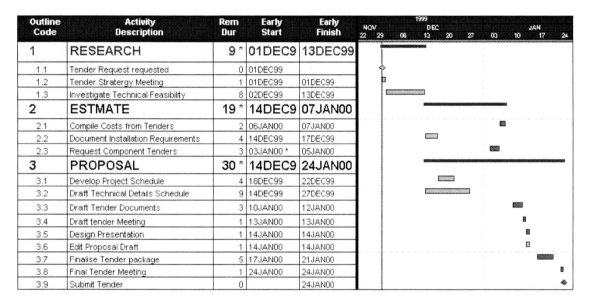

Outline Code	Activity Description	Rem Dur	Early Start	Early Finish
1	RESEARCH	9 *	01DEC9	13DEC99
1.1	Tender Request requested	0	01DEC99	
1.2	Tender Stratergy Meeting	1	01DEC99	01DEC99
1.3	Investigate Technical Feasibility	8	02DEC99	13DEC99
2	ESTMATE	19 *	14DEC9	07JAN00
2.1	Compile Costs from Tenders	2	06JAN00	07JAN00
2.2	Document Installation Requirements	4	14DEC99	17DEC99
2.3	Request Component Tenders	3	03JAN00 *	05JAN00
3	PROPOSAL	30 *	14DEC9	24JAN00
3.1	Develop Project Schedule	4	18DEC99	22DEC99
3.2	Draft Technical Details Schedule	9	14DEC99	27DEC99
3.3	Draft Tender Documents	3	10JAN00	12JAN00
3.4	Draft tender Meeting	1	13JAN00	13JAN00
3.5	Design Presentation	1	14JAN00	14JAN00
3.6	Edit Proposal Draft	1	14JAN00	14JAN00
3.7	Finalise Tender package	5	17JAN00	21JAN00
3.8	Final Tender Meeting	1	24JAN00	24JAN00
3.9	Submit Tender	0		24JAN00

Costs, Resources and logic may be applied to Topic Activities.

Activity Codes and Activity ID Codes are usually superior to Outlining as a method of organizing Activities. It is recommended that Outlining is only used when a Microsoft Project MPX file is opened to assist you in assigning activity codes.

It is suggested that you use Activity Codes in preference to Topic Activities as they provide a far more flexibility way of presenting your project.

13.3.1 Creating and Using Topic Activities

A Topic activity is created by **Indenting** subordinate activities.

- A maximum of ten levels of Outlining are available.

- Codes need not be defined before Outlining commences.

To create a **Topic Activity** create a Layout and Organize by **Outline**.

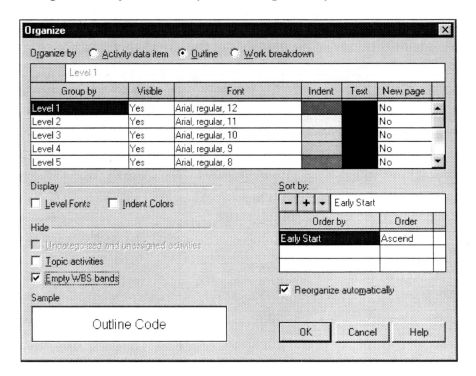

- Return to bar chart.

- Select one or more activities below the activity to become a Topic Activity.

- Use **Insert, Indent** or **Tab** or click the ⊞ icon on the toolbar to indent an activity and **Insert, Outdent** or **Shift Tab** or click the ⊞ icon on the toolbar to outdent an activity.

- The activity above the indented activity becomes a topic activity.

- Further sub-levels of topic activities may be created and reversed in the same way.

- Topic activities may be hidden using the **Hide, Topic activities** check box in the **Organize** form.

13.3.2 Summarizing Topic Activities

Summarizing activities hides all the lower level activities under Topic Activity. Levels may be summarized or rolled up by:

- Double clicking in the Columns area on the Topic Activity you wish to summarize

- Selecting Format, Summarization and Expand or Summarize All

- Using the **Collapse** or **Expand** options under **Summarize All** icon 🔲

- Using the **Collapse** 🔲 or **Expand** 🔲 icons.

13.3.3 Differences Between MS Project and SureTrak Outdent and Indent

There are differences in how MS Project and SureTrak treat logic links when using Indent and Outdent. MS Project changes logic when indenting activities and will remove a predecessor from the first Activity and place it on the new Topic Activity. SureTrak will not change logic, but give a warning message. The operator has to sort out the logic issues when indenting in SureTrak.

 In SureTrak predecessors applied to topic activities are predecessors of all the child activities but are not shown in the predecessor box. It is good practice to apply predecessors only to activities that are not topic activities.

It is recommended you use the activity codes to group the activities as it is far more flexible than Outlining.

14 OPTIONS AND OUT OF SEQUENCE PROGRESS

14.1 Options

The **Options** forms allow you to decide how SureTrak calculates and displays information. Most of the options are self-explanatory. Under **Tools, Options,** there are six tabs:

- Project

- Resource

- General

- Defaults

- View

- File Locations

This chapter will explain the functions of each function form.

14.1.1 Project

This information was covered in the chapter **CREATING A PROJECT AND SETTING UP THE SOFTWARE**. To recap:

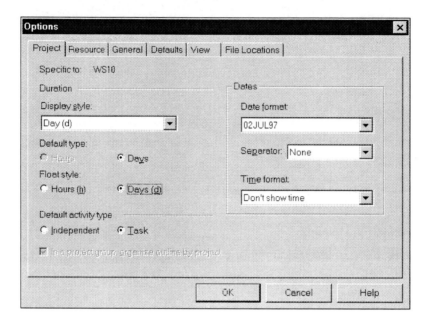

Duration

- **Display Style** is the format used in the bar chart columns. Select Days unless more detailed planning is required.

- **Default Type** specifies the format in which durations may be entered and how they are displayed on the screen. If **Days** is selected as the default, then a duration entered as 2 will give a 2 day duration activity. A 2 hour duration activity should be entered as 2h.

- **Float Style** is the display format for float.

Default Activity Type

- This should be set as **Task** unless advanced resourcing calculations are required.

Date and **Time Format** are the formats used to display dates and time.

 To avoid the confusion between the numerical US date style, (mmddyy) and the numerical European date style, (ddmmyy) you should adopt the ddmmmyy style as displayed above, 02JUL97. For example in the USA 020797 is read as 07 Feb 97 and in most other countries as 02 Jul 97.

14.1.2 Resource

These options affect how the software calculates percentages, Remaining Durations and costs during statusing.

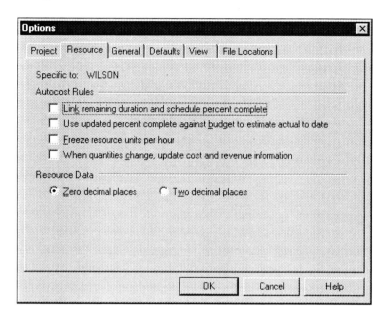

These options are covered in more detail in the chapter **STATUSING PROJECTS WITH RESOURCES**.

14.1.3 General

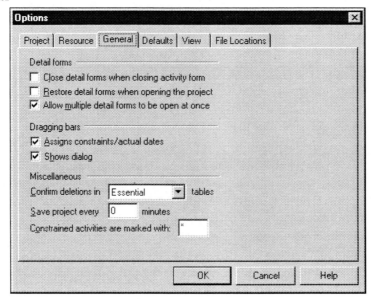

Details Form

These options dictate which forms are left open or closed when editing activities. It is suggested the above are used as defaults.

Dragging Bars

SureTrak allows the user to click on a bar, hold the mouse button down and move the activity forward or backward in time.

- Select **Assign constraints/actual dates** below **Dragging Bars** if you wish to have the ability to set a constraint after you have dragged the bar. The constraint will be either:

  ➢ **Start no earlier than** when the activity is moved forward in time or backward in time

  ➢ An **Actual start** if moved backward in time to past the data date.

- **Shows dialog** will display a dialog box confirming your wish to set the constraint or actual start.

Miscellaneous

Confirm deletions in tables enables you to be prompted when deleting items from tables. Deletions from tables may not be undone

If **Save project** is set then the project is automatically saved. When set to zero the project is not auto saved.

You can mark **constrained activities** using any symbol or alphanumeric character. It is suggested that the * symbol (Shift 8 on many keyboards) is used. The constraint is displayed next to the date e.g. 01DEC99 * .

14.1.4 Defaults

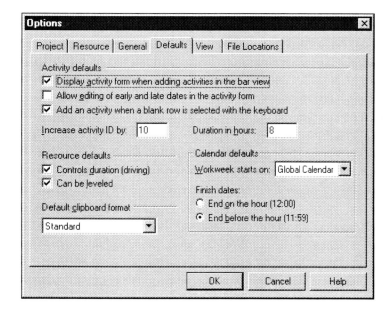

Activity defaults

- **Display activity form when adding activities in bar view** displays the activity form when adding activities. This is useful for adding information about the new activities.

- **Allow editing of early and late dates in activity form**. This allows editing of dates in the activity form when manual calculation is selected in the **Tools**, **Schedule** form. These are reset when the schedule is recalculated

- **Add an activity when a blank row is selected with the keyboard.** This inserts a new activity when a blank row is selected either with the keyboard or the mouse.

- **Increase activity ID by** allows you to nominate the number by which new Activity IDs are increased.

- **Duration in hours** specifies the duration that new activities are assigned.

Resource defaults

These options are covered in more detail in the chapter **STATUSING PROJECTS WITH RESOURCES**.

Calendar Defaults

This section allows editing of the calendar defaults. It is recommended that the above are used as defaults.

- **Workweek starts on:** specifies the day that is displayed in the timescale when it is set to weeks.

14.1.5 View

View alters some of the display defaults:

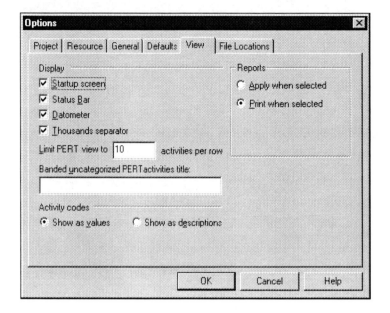

Display

These check boxes allow you to display or hide the:

- **Startup screen** (not covered in this book)

- Status bar

- Datometer

- Thousands separator

- and

- **Limit PERT view to ?? activities per row** allows you to limit the number of activities per row for display purposes.

- **Band uncategorized PERT activities title:** enable you to assign a title for unassigned activities in the **PERT**, **Organize**, **Group by** option.

Reports

You have the option of applying the report formatting or printing a report when one is applied using **Tools**, **Reports**, **Apply**.

Activity Codes

Activity codes or their descriptions may be displayed in the columns. When descriptions are displayed then the column data may not be edited.

14.1.6 File Locations

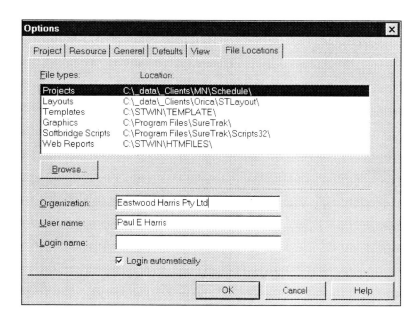

This option allows you to select the default directories for SureTrak data. The settings allow you to nominate where you have your data files stored in your computer and may be changed when you wish. For example, this feature allows you to keep more than one set of layouts, each in a different directory.

Login Name/Login Automatically

Type your login name and mark the Login Automatically checkbox to have SureTrak automatically log in to project group and Concentric (P3) type projects.

14.2 Out of Sequence Progress and Open Ends

Select **Tools**, **Schedule** to display the **Schedule** form.

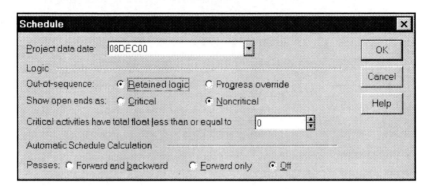

14.2.1 Out of Sequence Progress

Out-of-sequence Progress decides how original logic applies to the remaining work of a partially completed activity.

The effect of selecting **Retained logic** where any remaining work on an activity is scheduled to be completed after the predecessor is shown below:

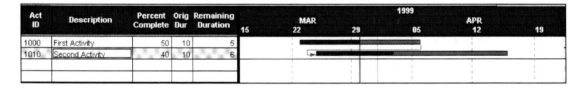

The effect of **Progress override** where any remaining work continues uninterrupted and ignores the predecessor logic is shown below:

14.2.2 Open Ends

An open end is an activity without a successor. You may choose to display activities as **Critical** or **Non Critical**. It is suggested that open end activities are always displayed as critical as a reminder that they are a potential problem.

WORKSHOP 18

Out of Sequence

Assignment

1. Create a new project called Workshop 18 with today's date as the start date.

2. Add two 10 day duration activities.

3. Link them with a FS relationship.

4. Update progress by one week.

5. Mark the successor activity with an Actual Start Date the same as the predecessor activity.

6. Test the Schedule Retained logic and Progress override options and note the impact.

7. Close the new project after saving.

15 CREATING AND USING RESOURCES

A resource may be defined as something or someone that is assigned to an activity and is required to complete the task. This includes people or groups of people, materials, plant, access and money.

It is recommended that you assign the minimum number of resources to activities. Avoid cluttering the schedule with resources that are in plentiful supply or are of little importance.

The following steps should be followed to create and use resources in a SureTrak schedule:

- Create your resources in the Resource Dictionary

- Assign the resources to activities

- Manipulate the resource calendar if resources have special timing requirements

15.1 Creating Resources

Select **Define**, **Resources** to add resources to the resource dictionary.

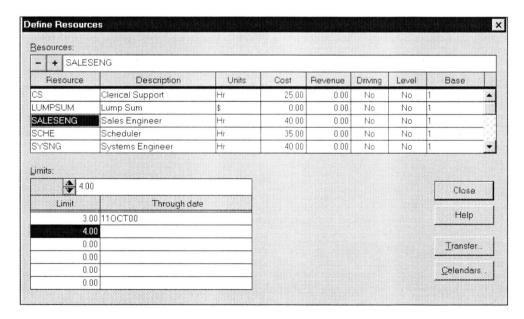

- Use the ⊡ icon to insert a new resource.

- Enter the **Resource** code, up to 8 characters long.

- Enter the **Description**, up to 40 characters.

- Enter the **Units**, eg: Hrs, Days, up to 4 characters.

- Enter the **Cost** if you wish to calculate the cost and/or monitor cost of the resource.

- Enter the **Revenue** if you wish to calculate the revenue that will be generated by the resource.

- **Driving** When **No** is selected, resources are assigned to activities as Non-driving. They may be changed to Driving after assignment. If **Yes** is selected then the reverse applies.

- **Level** When this option is set to **No** the resource is assigned to an activity as not requiring leveling. When **Yes** the Resource is leveled. This option may be changed at any time after the resource has been assigned.

- **Base** is the calendar used as the default for the resource. The resource calendar stays the same as the Base calendar until it is modified.

- **Limit** and **Through date** nominate the number of resources available up to the date on the first line. The second line nominates the number of resources available between the date on the first and second lines. The picture above shows there are 3 Market Surveyors up to 11 Oct 2000 and 4 after 11 Oct 2000.

- **Transfer** allows transferring Resources from another project.

- **Calendars** allow defining Resource calendars for individual resources. This is used for defining individual holidays, etc.

15.2 Driving and Non-driving Resources

Driving Resources determine the duration of an activity and Non-driving resources do not.

When all resources assigned to an activity are nominated as Non-driving, the duration of the activity is determined by the duration nominated in the Activity form.

When a resource is nominated as a Driving Resource then the duration of the Resource entered in the Resource Form determines the duration of the activity. When there is more than one Driving Resource, the duration of the longest resource determines the duration of the activity.

 Driving Resources add a further level of complexity to the schedule. Avoid using Driving Resources until you have experience in using SureTrak and the specific requirements of the schedule dictate that you should use them.

WORKSHOP 19

Defining Resources

Preamble

As we have statused our project, we need to revert to the un-progressed program we saved prior to statusing the current schedule. The resources must now be added to this schedule.

Assignment

1. Close your WILSON project.

2. Open WILSON01 and then save it as WILSON. Overwrite the existing project when prompted.

3. Set your Default Options so that Resource Defaults are not Driving, do not Level and the Resource Option so that Resource data is calculated to two decimal places.

4. Add the following resources to the project by defining them in the resource dictionary.

Resource	Description	Units	Cost	Driving	Limit
BM	Bid Manager	Hr	50.00	No	1.00
CS	Clerical Support	Hr	25.00	No	2.00
LUMPSUM	Lump Sum	$	0.00	No	0.00
SALESENG	Sales Engineer	Hr	40.00	No	1.00
SCHED	Scheduler	Hr	25.00	No	1.00
SYSENG	Systems Engineer	Hr	40.00	No	2.00

Note: Use the default values of **No** for Level and **5** for Base.

15.3 Assigning Resources to Activities

When a resource is assigned to an activity it has three principal components:

- **Quantity**, such as hours, days, weights or lengths

- Cost

- **Revenue** which is the expected income

Each component has its own Form.

- The **Quantity** component of the resource which is displayed in the **Resource** form

- The **Cost** component which is displayed in the **Cost** form

- The **Revenue** component which is displayed in the **Revenue** form

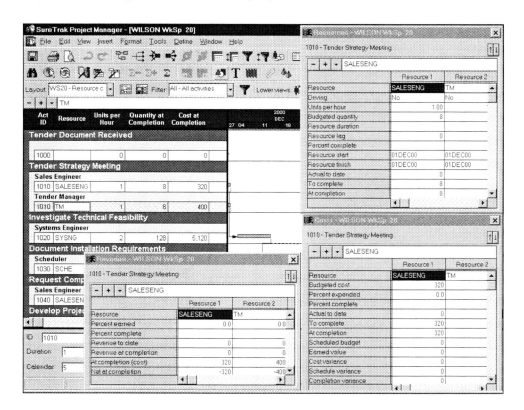

The resource data may be displayed in all three forms when a Resource is assigned to an activity. Quantities or Costs may be zero if they are not assigned a value.

The Budget Quantity and Cost are set to equal the At Completion when a Resource is assigned to an activity.

Resources may be assigned to activities using one of the following methods:

- Insert Resource Assignment form

- Resource form

- Costs form

15.3.1 Assigning Resources Using Insert Resource Assignment Form

Highlight the activity you wish to assign a resource to. Select **Insert**, **Resource Assignment** or click the ![] icon on the toolbar to display the **Insert Resource Assignment** form.

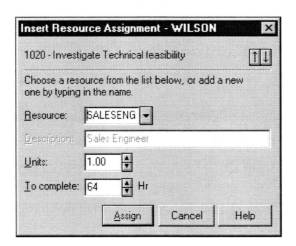

- Select the **Resource** from the drop-down box.

- Nominate the number of **Units**, this could be the number of people working on a task.

- Select the total quantity **To complete**, this could be the total number of hours required to complete a task.

- Click **Assign**.

- You may then assign another resource to a task or use the arrows in the top right hand corner to move to the next or previous task.

You may also assign one or more resources against multiple activities by highlighting the activities you wish to assign the resource against before selecting **Insert**, **Resource Assignment** or clicking the ![] icon. You are then able to nominate the **Units** of the resource that will be assigned against each activity.

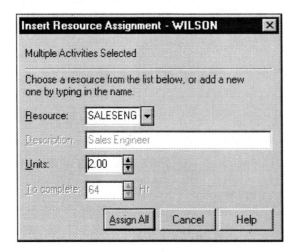

15.3.2 Assigning Resources Using Resource Form

Select **View**, **Activity Detail**, **Resources** to open the **Resources** form.

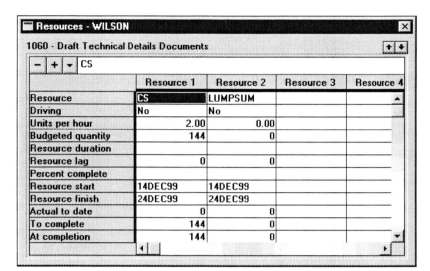

- Click into **Resource** and select the resource from the drop-down box at the top.

- **Driving Yes** or **No** will be copied from the default set in the Resource Dictionary. It may be changed on assignment or at a later date.

- **Units per hour** is the quantity of work per time period.

- **Budget quantity** equals **Duration** multiplied by **Units per Hour**.

- **Budget quantity** is set to equal **To Complete** on assignment.

- **Resource duration** and **Resource lag** are used to define the resources relationship within the activity.

The remaining options are used when updating a schedule.

- **Percent Complete** is the percent of Budget quantity used when **Actual to date** is entered.

- **Actual to date** is the quantity consumed to date.

- **To complete** is the estimate of quantity to complete the task.

- **At completion** is the sum of **Actual to date** plus **To complete**.

- Entering **At completion** will calculate **To complete** and entering **To complete** will calculate **At completion**.

- Completion variance is Budget minus At completion.

- **Costs** are calculated using the rates in the Resource Dictionary.

15.3.3 Assigning Resources Using Costs Form

The Costs form may be used for assigning resources to Activities when there are no hours or quantities associated with the activity.

Select **View**, **Activity Detail**, **Costs** to display the resource cost in the Resource form.

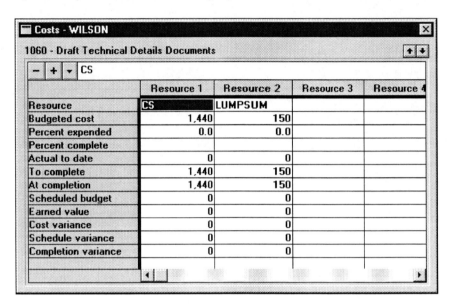

- The resource may be assigned from this form in the same way as the **Resources** form. This form is usually used for assigning resources that do not have quantities, such as Lump Sum costs.

- Normally you would enter the **Budget cost** and SureTrak will set the **To complete** and the **At completion** to equal the Budget cost.

The remaining options are used when updating a schedule

- Percent expended is proportion of Budget Spent, when Actual to date is entered.

- **At completion** equals **Actual to date** plus **To complete**. Either **At completion** or **To complete** may be entered and the other will be calculated.

- **Scheduled Budget**, **Earned Value**, **Cost Variance**, **Schedule Variance** and **Completion Variance** are used when the schedule is statused.

 You are advised to remove the quantities (using the Resource form) after adding Lump Sum items to avoid the quantities being included in histograms and tables based on quantities. It is recommend that you add quantity based resources from the Resource form instead of the Cost form.

WORKSHOP 20

Preamble

The resources must now be assigned to the specific tasks they will work on.

Assignment

1. Remove all Grauping and sort by Activity ID.
2. Using both the Resource Detail and Insert Resource Assingment forms assign the resources to the following activities (Lump Sum resources must be added using the Cost Detail form and any quantities against Lump Sums deleted in the Resource form).

Act ID	Resource	Units per Hour	Quantity at Completion	Cost at Completion
1010	BM	1	8	400
1010	SALESENG	1	8	320
1020	SYSNG	2	128	5,120
1030	SCHED	1	32	800
1040	SALESENG	1	24	960
1050	SCHED	1	32	800
1060	CS	2	144	3,600
1060	LUMPSUM	0	0	1,500
1070	SALESENG	1	16	640
1080	BM	1	24	1,200
1090	BM	1	8	400
1090	SALESENG	1	8	320
1100	BM	1	8	400
1100	SALESENG	1	8	320
1100	SYSENG	1	8	320
1110	BM	1	8	400
1120	BM	1	32	1,600
1120	LUMPSUM	0	0	2,500
1130	BM	1	8	400
1130	SALESENG	1	8	320

3. Format your columns to reflect above.

4. Group the data by Project, Activity ID and Resource with a Total on the Project line.

5. Check your data entry with the picture over.

6. Save layout as WS20, Resource Entry Check.

7. Save your project.

Act ID	Activity Description	Orig Dur	Resource	Units per Hour	Quantity at Completion	Cost at Completion
Wilson WkSp 20 - Bid Programme for Wilson Bedding						
		39		20.00	512.00	22,320.00
1000 - Bid Request Documents Received						
1000	Bid Request Documents Received	0		0.00	0.00	0.00
1010 - Bid Strategy Meeting						
BM - Bid Manager						
1010	Bid Strategy Meeting	1	BM	1.00	8.00	400.00
SALESENG - Sales Engineer						
1010	Bid Strategy Meeting	1	SALESENG	1.00	8.00	320.00
1020 - Investigate Technical Feasibility						
SYSENG - Systems Engineer						
1020	Investigate Technical Feasibility	8	SYSENG	2.00	128.00	5,120.00
1030 - Document Installation Requirements						
SCHED - Scheduler						
1030	Document Installation Requirements	4	SCHED	1.00	32.00	800.00
1040 - Request Component Tenders						
SALESENG - Sales Engineer						
1040	Request Component Tenders	3	SALESENG	1.00	24.00	960.00
1050 - Develop Project Schedule						
SCHED - Scheduler						
1050	Develop Project Schedule	4	SCHED	1.00	32.00	800.00
1060 - Draft Technical Details Schedule						
CS - Clerical Support						
1060	Draft Technical Details Schedule	9	CS	2.00	144.00	3,600.00
LUMPSUM - Lump Sum						
1060	Draft Technical Details Schedule	9	LUMPSUM	0.00	0.00	1,500.00
1070 - Compile Costs from Component Bids						
SALESENG - Sales Engineer						
1070	Compile Costs from Component Bids	2	SALESENG	1.00	16.00	640.00
1080 - Draft the Bid Document						
BM - Bid Manager						
1080	Draft the Bid Document	3	BM	1.00	24.00	1,200.00
1090 - Meeting to review the Draft Bid Document						
BM - Bid Manager						
1090	Meeting to review the Draft Bid	1	BM	1.00	8.00	400.00
SALESENG - Sales Engineer						
1090	Meeting to review the Draft Bid	1	SALESENG	1.00	8.00	320.00
1100 - Design Presentation						
BM - Bid Manager						
1100	Design Presentation	1	BM	1.00	8.00	400.00
SALESENG - Sales Engineer						
1100	Design Presentation	1	SALESENG	1.00	8.00	320.00
SYSENG - Systems Engineer						
1100	Design Presentation	1	SYSENG	1.00	8.00	320.00
1110 - Edit Proposal Draft Bid Document						
BM - Bid Manager						
1110	Edit Proposal Draft Bid Document	1	BM	1.00	8.00	400.00
1120 - Negotiate Component Work Packages						
BM - Bid Manager						
1120	Negotiate Component Work Packages	4	BM	1.00	32.00	1,600.00
LUMPSUM - Lump Sum						
1120	Negotiate Component Work Packages	4	LUMPSUM	0.00	0.00	2,500.00
1130 - Final Review of Bid Document						
BM - Bid Manager						
1130	Final Review of Bid Document	1	BM	1.00	8.00	400.00
SALESENG - Sales Engineer						
1130	Final Review of Bid Document	1	SALESENG	1.00	8.00	320.00
1140 - Submit Bid						
1140	Submit Bid	0		0.00	0.00	0.00

15.4 Editing and Using Resource Calendars

Base Calendars are applied to activities but they may not accommodate specific resource requirements. For example, when a person goes on holidays or is occupied on another project.

Resource Calendars should be used when resources have a unique availability.

When a resource is created, a unique resource calendar is created automatically. This is a copy of the base calendar that is selected when the resource is created. This resource calendar may be modified if required.

15.4.1 Editing a Resource Calendar

The resource calendar may be edited by selecting either:

- Define Calendars, Resource tab or

- Define Resources, Calendars.

All edits to the calendars are performed in the same manner as the Base calendars.

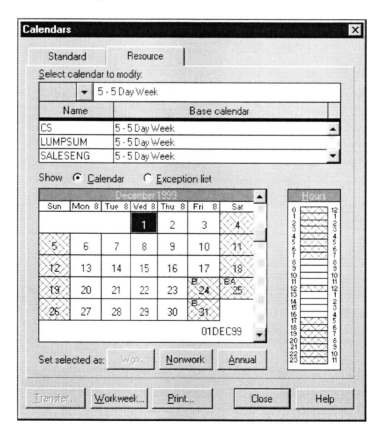

- **Exception List** displays holidays and is edited in the same way as Base calendars.

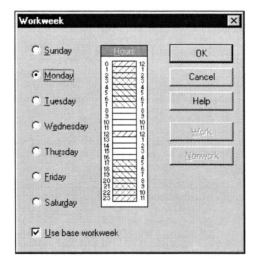

- **Workweek** displays the work week and is edited in the same way as Base calendars.

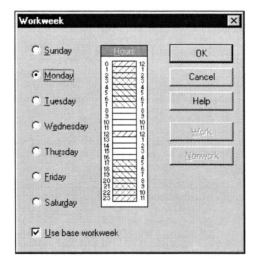

15.4.2 Using a Resource Calendar to Calculate Durations

A resource calendar will only be used in calculating Finish dates when the **Activity Type** is assigned as **Independent** or **Meeting**. When the activity is assigned an Activity Type of **Task** it then uses the activity Base calendar to calculate the finish date.

16 USING ACTIVITY TYPES AND DRIVING RESOURCES

There are eight **Activity Types** in SureTrak. Activity Types exist to enable the scheduler to more closely simulate real life situations. The Activity Types have their own rules for calculation and should be completely understood by the user before being used.

Some Activity Types have restrictions on the constraints they may use. For example, a Finish Milestone may not have a Start Date constraint.

The Activity Types are:

- Task
- Independent
- Meeting
- Start Milestone
- Finish Milestone
- Hammock
- WBS
- Topic

16.1 Assigning Activity Type to an Activity

Activity Types may be assigned by:

- Selecting the required **Type** from the **Act. Type** drop-down box in the **Activity** form (or typing in the first letter of the **Type** into the **Act. Type** drop-down box) or

- Displaying a column with Activity Type and updating the column.

16.2 Task Activity Type

Task Activity Type is used for scheduling normal activities. The Activity always utilizes the calendar assigned in the Activity form for calculation of dates and durations.

When an activity is nominated as a Task, the Resource ignores its Resource Calendar, irrespective of whether the Resource is Non-driving or Driving.

 It is recommended that the Activity Type of **Task** is used for all work except when specific scheduling requirements dictate the need for another Activity Type.

16.3 Independent

An Activity should be made Independent when you wish to schedule a resource using the resource calendar to determine the activity duration and end dates.

The Resource should be set to **Driving** when assigned to an Independent activity.

- A Resource set to **Non-driving** may be scheduled by SureTrak outside the activity duration, and therefore, provide a result that is not logical. When an activity is changed from **Task** to **Independent**, SureTrak will change a **Non-driving** Resource to **Driving**.

- Activity Start dates will be the earliest of all its **Driving** Resources and **End dates** the latest of its **Driving** Resources.

- The resource **Lag** is the delay from the start of an activity to when a resource starts working. Therefore, if one resource is assigned to an activity with a lag then the **Lag** plus the **Duration** determines the duration of the activity.

- An Independent Activity Resource may work independently from other resources, therefore, it may work on an activity when other resources assigned to the Activity are not available due to their own calendars.

16.4 Meeting

These are similar to Independent Activities but all resources must be available based on their own Resource Calendars for the Activity to have the work scheduled.

- All the resources must be **Driving** for **Meeting** Activities to calculate properly.

- When changing an Activity from **Task** to **Meeting** to **Independent** then **Non-driving** Activities are changed to **Driving**.

The following diagram shows how SureTrak schedules Task, Independent and Meeting Activities.

2 Day Activity	Day 1	Day 2	Day 3	Day 4	Day 5	Day 6	Day 7
Calendar for Resource 1			▓	▓			
Calendar for Resource 2	▓						
Calendar for Resource 3	▓	▓			▓		
Activity 1 – Task	██	██					
Activity 2 – Independent	██	██	██	██			
Activity 3 – Meeting						██	██

16.5 Start Milestone

A Start Milestone has no duration and is often used to indicate the start of a major event.

- It only has a Start Date.

- It has to be statused or it will remain in front of the data date.

- Constraints that are not allowed are grayed out in the constraints box.

16.6 Finish Milestone

A Finish Milestone has no duration and is often used to indicate the end of a major event.

- It only has a Finish Date.

- It has to be statused or it will remain in front of the data date.

- Constraints that are not allowed are grayed out in the constraints box.

16.7 Hammock

A Hammock is used to summarize the duration of a group of activities. It does not summarize costs or resources and is independent of the activity coding of the activities it is summarizing.

To create a Hammock

- From the Activity Detail Form select Activity Type **Hammock**.

- Create Start to Start Predecessor relationships to one or more activities that dictate the start of the Hammock.

- Create Finish to Finish Successor relationships to one or more activities that dictate the finish of the Hammock.

Resources and costs may be assigned to Hammocks.

 Be careful with setting the Auto Cost Rules. When the resource is made Non-driving and units per hour are frozen, the Quantity to complete will increase when the Hammock duration is increased. When a resource is made Driving it ignores the duration of the Hammock for scheduling the work.

16.8 Topic

Topic Activities are created when Outlining is used. This subject is discussed under Outlining in the **ORGANIZING ACTIVITIES** chapter.

Resources assigned to Topic Activities calculate as follows:

- When assigned as **Non-driving** adopt the duration of the activity.

- When the **Resource Unit Per Hour** is frozen, an increase in activity duration will increase the quantity and cost.

- When the Resource is **Driving** then the resource is effectively scheduled separately from the Task.

17 RESOURCE LEVELING

Resource Leveling is a SureTrak function allowing the optimization of resource use by delaying activities until resources become available and thus reduce the peaks in resource requirements. This feature may extend the length of a project should you choose to use this option.

The leveling function should be only be employed by novice users with extreme caution. It requires the scheduler to have a very good understanding of how SureTrak operates. Leveling increases the complexity of a schedule and requires a different approach to the construction of a schedule. Leveling requires the user to have a solid understanding of how SureTrak resourcing functions calculate before attempting to use leveling.

Your ability to understand how SureTrak operates is important for you to be able to utilize the leveling function with confidence on larger schedules. It is recommended that you practice with small simple schedules to gain experience in leveling and develop an understand the leveling issues before attempting leveling a complex schedule.

This chapter will outline the SureTrak Resource Leveling functions including:

- Resource **Level** form,

- **Resource** form,

- Guidelines on Leveling and

- What to look for if resources are not leveling.

17.1 Level Form

The **Leveling** form allows you to nominate most of the Leveling prerequisites. Select **Tools, Level…** to open the **Level** form:

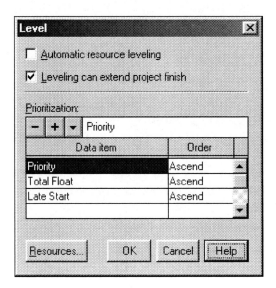

- **Automatic resource leveling** - levels the schedule each time the schedule is recalculated.

- **Leveling can extend the project finish**:
  - ➤ When checked leveling will allow activities to extend beyond a **Must finish date**, when assigned in the **Project Overview** form, or beyond the latest date calculated by the schedule.
  - ➤ When unchecked the activities will only be delayed until all float is consumed and leveling will not extend the finish date of the project beyond a **Must finish date**, when assigned in the **Project Overview** form, or beyond the latest date calculated by the schedule when no **Must finish date** is assigned.

- **Prioritization:** is used to set leveling the priorities and activities are assigned resources in according to the Data item nominated in the first line, if two activities have the same value in the first line then the priority in the second line is used. The Activity ID is the final value used to assign resources. There are many options for leveling and the following are some options you may consider:
  - ➤ **Priority** is a SureTrak field that may be set from 0 to 999, the default is 1. If the priority is set to 0 then the resources in the activity will not be leveled. Those with a priority 1 will be assigned resources first. This field is not acknowledged in P3, however an Activity Code may be shared by both systems with the same result.
  - ➤ **Activity Codes** or **Activity ID Codes** may be used to level.
  - ➤ **Remaining Duration, Early Start, Total Float** and **Late Start** may be selected and used in conjunction with the **Order** option of **Ascending** or **Descending**.

- The **Resources** option opens the **Resource** form where you may select which resources are leveled, see the next section for details.

17.2 Resources Form

You should select the resources to be leveled from the **Resources** form. The form below indicates that the Sales Engineer is the only resource that will be leveled and there are a maximum of 2 available up to 05JAN04 and 3 after 05JAN04.

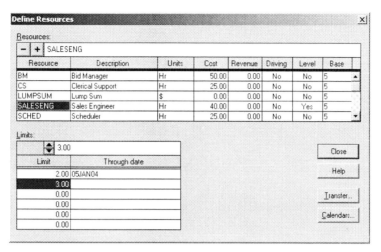

All the pictures below display three activities assigned with one resource **DESENG** and the activities have been set with a priority of 10, 30 and 20.

The picture below displays the schedule unleveled and the histogram showing the resource is overloaded:

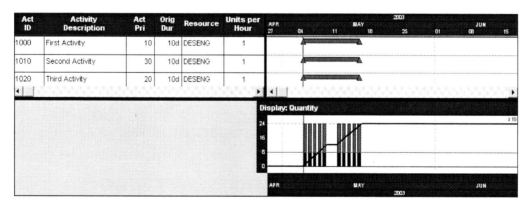

After Leveling by selecting **Tools, Level Now** or pressing **Shift + F9** the activities have been delayed according to Priority and the resource is no longer overloaded:

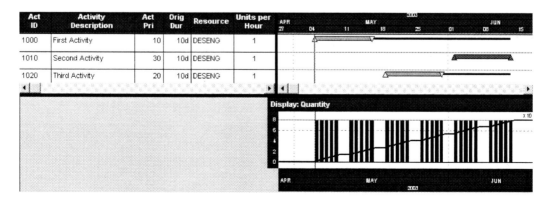

In the picture below the project has a **Must finish by**: of date of 1JUN0302 which has been set in the **Project Overview** form. The tasks float is calculated to this date, and the resource is overloaded as observed in the histogram below:

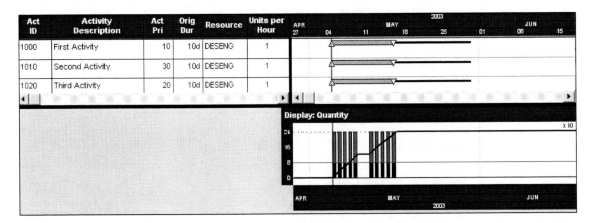

When the option **Leveling can extend the project finish**: is checked, activity 1010 is scheduled beyond the imposed project finish date and generates negative float:

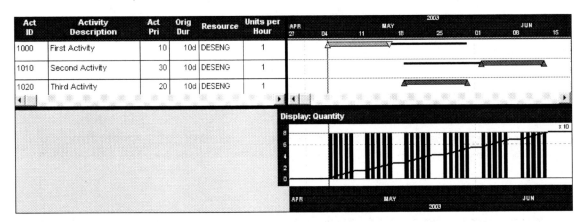

When the option **Leveling can extend the project finish**: is unchecked, activity 1010 is not scheduled beyond the imposed project finish date, the project is completed within the project imposed finish date and the resource remains overloaded but overloading is reduced:

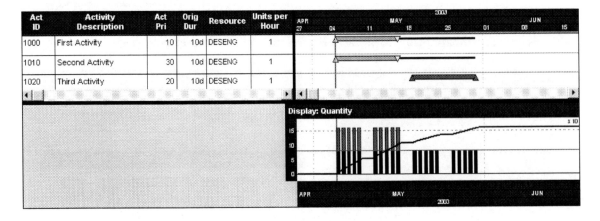

17.3 Guidelines for Leveling

Leveling a schedule is a skill that is acquired through practice and experience and there are a few fundamentals that a user must bear in mind before attempting to level a complex schedule.

- If you are not an experienced scheduling software user then it is strongly suggested that you obtain some serious experience in using SureTrak with resources before attempting to use leveling on a complex schedule, especially if you are going to attempt to level a progressed schedule. You will need this experience to be able to resolve some of the complex issues that are often presented when attempting to level a schedule.

- You need to approach the structure of the schedule differently from the beginning of schedule construction. Without leveling schedulers normally apply soft logic (sequencing logic) to prevent a number of activities occurring at the same time. Should leveling be considered as a method of scheduling then the soft logic should be omitted from the beginning of the construction of the schedule.

- All users and reviewers of the schedule must understand that a leveled schedule may dramatically change with the addition or removal or change to activities or change in priorities.

- There are some principals that should be considered when leveling:
  - ➢ Only level resources that are overloaded and you are unable to supplement easily or have an absolute limit.
  - ➢ Try leveling one resource at a time and view the histograms making sure each resource is leveling. If a resource is not leveling and overload remains displayed in the histograms you will need to go through the check list over the page and level again.
  - ➢ Once all resources are leveling individually then you should start leveling with two resources and then three. Do not start leveling with all the resources at once as the schedule will often do some drastic things and extend the project end date unrealistically.
  - ➢ Don't expect a perfect result and be satisfied with an average resource usage that meets your requirements over periods such as months and sort out small peaks in future resource requirement nearer to the start of the activity.

- Activities have the following options which affect how the duration is calculated:
  - ➢ Activity Types of Task, Independent or Meeting.
  - ➢ Resources assigned to Activities may be are Driving or Non Driving or both.
  - ➢ Resources may have their own calendars.

To understand how leveling will delay or change durations of activities you will need to be aware of which of the above combinations you have employed in your schedule, and you will then need to understand how each combination calculates under a non leveling environment. You will then appreciate how the durations of Independent and Meeting activities are calculated and what the effect leveling may have on their durations.

17.4 What to Look for if Resources are not Leveling

- Have you selected a resource to level in the Resources form? The resources to be leveled must be selected in the Resource form.

- Have you set the Limits in the Resource Dictionary? A resource needs a limit to level.

- A resource will not be leveled when you assign a resource to an activity with a Units per time period greater than value set in the resource dictionary. This may occur when:

  ➢ The **Resource Limit** in the **Resource Dictionary** is reduced, or

  ➢ A Task has been assigned a resource with a **Unit per Time Period** that is greater than the **Limit**, or

  ➢ When the **Freeze Units per Time Period** is unchecked and the duration of an activity has been reduced thus increasing the assigned **Units per time period** over the maximum available in the **Resource** form.

- Have you assigned a Mandatory constraint to an unleveled task? Tasks with a Mandatory constraint will not be leveled.

- Have you checked **Leveling can extend the project finish** option. This option allows activities without float to level.

WORKSHOP 21

Resources Leveling

Preamble

This exercise is independent of the Wilson Bedding schedule. We will recreate the example in this chapter.

Assignment

1. Create a schedule titled **Leveling**.
2. Give the schedule a five-day week calendar, Start date 5 May 2003 and Finish date 27 June 2003.
3. Create three activities called First Activity, Second Activity and Third Activity.
4. Create one resource called **RES**, **Resource** with a normal availability of 1 and a maximum availability of 1.
5. Assign the Priority as shown below.
6. Create the layout below showing the Early bar above and Total Float and Unleveled bar below.
7. Display the Resource Histogram.

Before Leveling

Act ID	Activity Description	Act Priority	Orig Dur
1000	First Activity	1	10d
1010	Second Activity	2	10d
1020	Third Activity	1	10d

After Leveling

Act ID	Activity Description	Act Priority	Orig Dur
1000	First Activity	1	10d
1010	Second Activity	2	10d
1020	Third Activity	1	10d

18 STATUSING PROJECTS WITH RESOURCES

Statusing a project with resources takes place in two distinct steps:

- The dates are statused using the methods outlined in the **TRACKING PROGRESS** chapter, then

- The resources are updated.

This chapter covers the following topics:

- Understanding Target Schedule and Budgets

- Understanding the Data Date with respect to resources

- Information Required to Update a Resourced Schedule

- Further techniques for Updating Dates and Percentage Complete

- Updating Resources

- Resource Histogram, S-Curves and Tables

18.1 Understanding Target Schedule and Budgets

Budgets

The Budget hours or quantities and costs of resources are automatically recorded in the Budget field of each resource as it is assigned to an activity.

 The Budget Costs and Quantities are always set equal to the **To Complete** until the activity has **Started**. This may be frustrating should you wish to show a revised estimate that is different from the Budget for unstarted activities.

Targets

A Target Schedule records the planned start and finish dates. The Target Dates are a copy of the current schedule dates that are copied into two fields:

- Target Start and

- Target Finish

Setting the Target dates was covered in the chapter **TRACKING PROGRESS**.

Target dates may be displayed using the following methods:

- Display the Target Start and Finish columns

- Display the Activity Detail, Dates form (shown below)

- Display the Bar Chart Bars

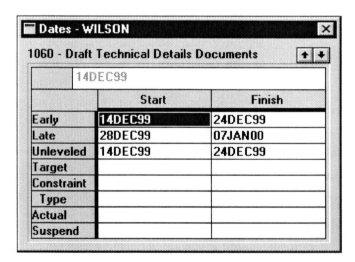

18.2 Understanding the Data Date

The **Data Date** is also known as **Review Date**, **Status Date**, **As Of Date** and **Update Date**.

- The **Data Date** is the date that divides past and future in the schedule.

- **Actual Costs** and **Quantities/Hours** should have occurred before the data date.

- Costs and Quantities/Hours To Complete occur after the data date.

- **Remaining durations** are calculated from the Data Date.

- The **Data Date** is not normally in the future, but often in the recent past, due to the time it may take to collect the information to status the schedule.

Formatting the Data Date

To format the Data Date display on the Bar Chart select **Format, Sight Lines** to display the **Sight Line** form.

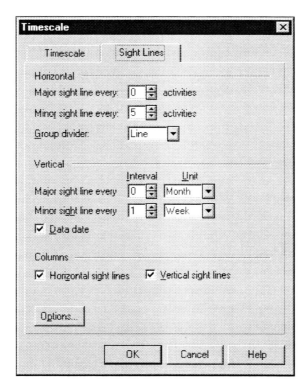

- Check the **Data Date** Box to display the Data Date in the Bar Chart Area.

- **Options** allow the selection of colors and line types for all sight lines.

- All other sight lines may be defined in this form.

18.3 Information Required to Update a Resourced Schedule

A project schedule is usually updated at the end of a period, such as each day, week or month. One of the purposes of updating a schedule is to establish differences between the plan and the current schedule.

The following information is required to status a resourced schedule.

Activities commenced in the update period:

- Actual Start date of the activity

- Remaining Duration from the status date or Expected Finish date

- Costs and Hours or Quantities to date

- Costs and Hours or Quantities to complete

- Suspend and Resume dates for activities that have had their work suspended

Activities Completed or Started and Completed in the update period:

- Actual Start date of the activity

- Actual Finish date of the activity

- Costs and Hours or Quantities to date

Activities Not Commenced:

- Changes in logic or date constraints

- Changes in Costs or Hours or Quantities

Once this information is collected the schedule may be updated.

18.4 Updating Dates and Percentage Complete

You should update the dates using the methods outlined in the chapter **TRACKING PROGRESS**. Two methods not covered earlier are:

- Using columns to status the dates

- Using bars to status the schedule

18.4.1 Using Columns to Status dates

A layout may be created with the columns required to status a project. You should display all the columns you wish to status.

- Actual Start and Actual Finish columns are available.

- If you wish to update **Resources** in columns then you will have to organize the layout by Resource.

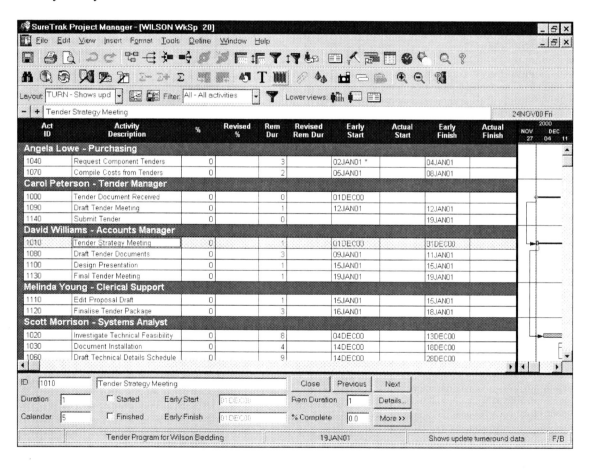

18.4.2 Updating Activities from the Bars in the Bar Chart

The **Update Progress** form may be accessed from the Activity Bar.

- The end of a bar is selected with the mouse.

- When the double arrow is displayed, press the **Shift** key and click the right mouse button and the pointer will change to a hammer & nail.

- Click the right mouse button and the **Update Progress** form is displayed.

18.5 Updating Resources

SureTrak has some options that allow the scheduler to decide how costs are calculated. These should be set before statusing the schedule for the first time.

18.5.1 Options, Resources

Select **Tools, Options, Resources** tab to nominate how SureTrak calculates the Resource data. It is important that these options are understood; they are well defined in SureTrak Help and the descriptions are self explanatory.

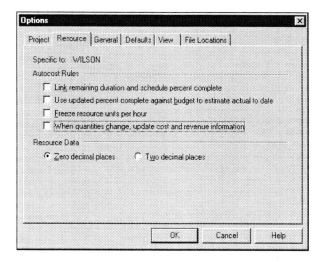

- Link remaining duration and scheduled percent complete was covered in detail in section 12.4.

- **Use update percent complete against budget to estimate actual to date** lets SureTrak calculate costs and quantities to date based on the percent complete and budget costs and quantities.

- Selecting **Freeze resource units per hour** results in an increase in **Quantities or Hours to complete** as the **Remaining Duration** is increased, and a decrease when the **Remaining Duration** is decreased. If this option is not selected then the **Quantity to Complete** remains constant and the **Units per hour** varies inversely to the **Remaining Duration**.

- Selecting **When quantities change, update cost and revenue information** allows SureTrak to calculate **Actual to date, To complete** and **At completion** from the Cost assigned to the resource in Define Resources. If this option is not selected the Costs are updated by the scheduler when Quantities change.

- **Resource Data** allows the costs and quantities to be calculated to zero or two decimal places.

 If at any time the Remaining Duration is set to Zero then the Hours/Quantity to complete is set to zero.

18.5.2 Updating Resources Using Resource and Costs Form

Select the Resources and/or Costs form to update the resource information.

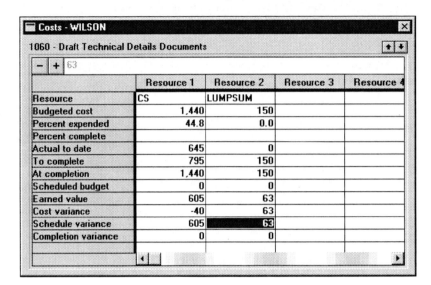

- The above example has the cost and quantities for **Actual to date** and **To complete** entered separately.

- **Scheduled Budget** is the amount of work planned to be completed by the data date.

- The **Earned Value** is the value of work completed to date, (i.e. % Comp x Budget).

- **Schedule variance** is the difference between the **Earned value** and **Scheduled budget**.

- **Completion variance** is the difference between **Budget cost** and **At completion**.

18.5.3 Updating Resources Using Columns

By selecting the **Layout by Resource** and the appropriate columns, the costs and quantities may be updated using the columns.

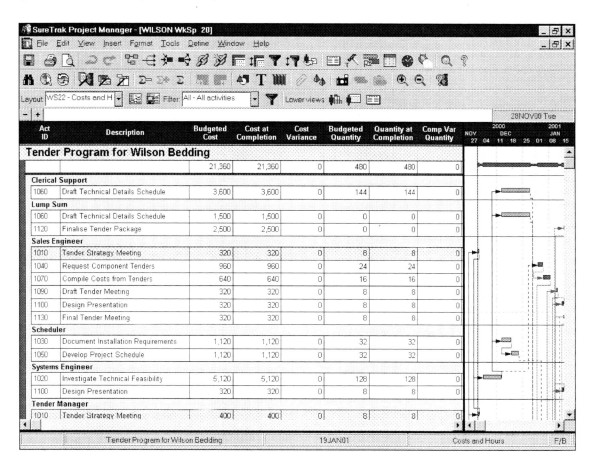

The layout must be organized by Resource to allow the editing of resource data in columns.

18.5.4 Updating Revenue

The Revenue is updated from the **Revenue** form.

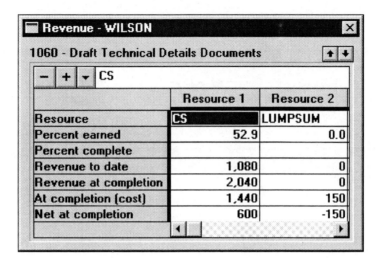

- **Revenue to date** is calculated from the **Quantity to date** multiplied by the **Revenue** as defined in the Resources dictionary.

- **Revenue at Completion** is calculated from the **Quantity at completion** multiplied by **Revenue** as defined in the Resources dictionary.

- **At Completion (cost)** is the same data as the **At completion** in the Cost form, and editing it here will change the Actual cost data.

- **Net at completion** equals **Revenue at completion** minus **At** completion (cost), i.e. the profit.

WORKSHOP 22

Updating Costs

Preamble

We need to status the activities and resources.

Assignment

1. Adjust the resource options as below.

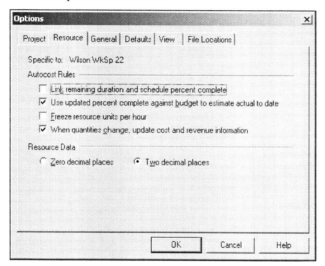

2. Store the Target dates.

3. Apply the Workshop 17 Layout.

4. Using the Progress Spotlight and Update Progress facility, update your project one week to the new data date of 08DEC03.

5. Update the Activity Percent Complete and Remaining using the Information below from the Task form using data below.

Act ID	Activity Description	Orig Dur	Early Start	Early Finish	Rem Dur	% Comp	2003
1000	Bid Request Documents Received	0	01DEC03		0	100	
1010	Bid Strategy Meeting	1	01DEC03	01DEC03 A	0	100	
1020	Investigate Technical Feasibility	8	02DEC03	15DEC03	6	60	
1030	Document Installation Requirements	4	16DEC03	19DEC03	4	0	
1040	Request Component Tenders	3	05JAN04	07JAN04	3	0	
1050	Develop Project Schedule	4	20DEC03	24DEC03	4	0	
1060	Draft Technical Details Schedule	9	16DEC03	30DEC03	9	0	

Continued over page

---

6. Create Layout WS22 titled Resource Data Entry by copying and editing WS20 the Resource Entry Chect layout.

Act ID	Activity Description	Orig Dur	Actual Quantity to Date	Quantity to Complete	Quantity at Completion	Completion Variance Quantity
	Wilson WkSp 22 - Bid Programme for Wilson Bedding					
		39	81.00	416.00	497.00	15.00
1000 - Bid Request Documents Received						
1000	Bid Request Documents Received	0	0.00	0.00	0.00	0.00
1010 - Bid Strategy Meeting						
BM - Bid Manager						
1010	Bid Strategy Meeting	1	8.00	0.00	8.00	0.00
SALESENG - Sales Engineer						
1010	Bid Strategy Meeting	1	10.00	0.00	10.00	-2.00
1020 - Investigate Technical Feasibility						
SYSENG - Systems Engineer						
1020	Investigate Technical Feasibility	8	63.00	48.00	111.00	17.00
1030 - Document Installation Requirements						
SCHED - Scheduler						
1030	Document Installation Requirements	4	0.00	32.00	32.00	0.00

7. Now Create Layout WS22b titled Costs and Hours Variance by copying WS22 and format the new layout as per the picture below, organized by Project with a Total at the Top.

Act ID	Activity Description	Budgeted Cost	Actual Cost to Date	Cost at Completion	Completion Variance Cost	Actual Quantity to Date	Quantity at Completion	Completion Variance Quantity
	Wilson WkSp 22 - Bid Programme for Wilson Bedding							
		22,320.00	3,320.00	21,720.00	600.00	81.00	497.00	15.00
1000	Bid Request Documents Received	0.00	0.00	0.00	0.00	0.00	0.00	0.00
1010	Bid Strategy Meeting	720.00	800.00	800.00	-80.00	18.00	18.00	-2.00
1020	Investigate Technical Feasibility	5,120.00	2,520.00	4,440.00	680.00	63.00	111.00	17.00
1030	Document Installation Requirements	800.00	0.00	800.00	0.00	0.00	32.00	0.00
1040	Request Component Tenders	960.00	0.00	960.00	0.00	0.00	24.00	0.00
1050	Develop Project Schedule	800.00	0.00	800.00	0.00	0.00	32.00	0.00
1060	Draft Technical Details Schedule	5,100.00	0.00	5,100.00	0.00	0.00	144.00	0.00
1070	Compile Costs from Component	640.00	0.00	640.00	0.00	0.00	16.00	0.00
1080	Draft the Bid Document	1,200.00	0.00	1,200.00	0.00	0.00	24.00	0.00
1090	Meeting to review the Draft Bid	720.00	0.00	720.00	0.00	0.00	16.00	0.00
1100	Design Presentation	1,040.00	0.00	1,040.00	0.00	0.00	24.00	0.00
1110	Edit Proposal Draft Bid Document	400.00	0.00	400.00	0.00	0.00	8.00	0.00
1120	Negotiate Component Work	4,100.00	0.00	4,100.00	0.00	0.00	32.00	0.00
1130	Final Review of Bid Document	720.00	0.00	720.00	0.00	0.00	16.00	0.00
1140	Submit Bid	0.00	0.00	0.00	0.00	0.00	0.00	0.00

This layout shows the current expenditure and forecast to complete is $600.00 less than budget and 15 hours lower than budget.

8. Now display the bars and review the progress.

18.6 Resource Histogram, S-Curves and Tables

Resource Histograms and S-Curves display the resource requirements in the lower portion of the screen in graphical or tabular format.

18.6.1 Resource Histogram

These are titled **Profiles** and may be displayed by selecting **View**, **Resource Profile** or **Ctrl F7**.

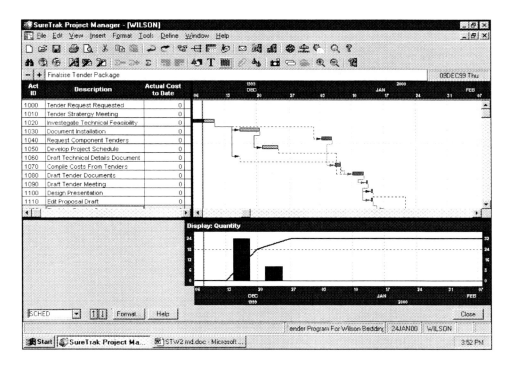

- Right click with the mouse over the histogram to see cumulative quantities or costs, and left click over the histogram to see periodic quantities or costs.

- **Format** is used to decide how the information is displayed.

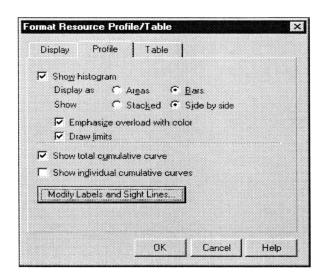

18.6.2 Resource Table

The Resource Table may be displayed by selecting **View**, **Resource Table** or **Shift F7**.

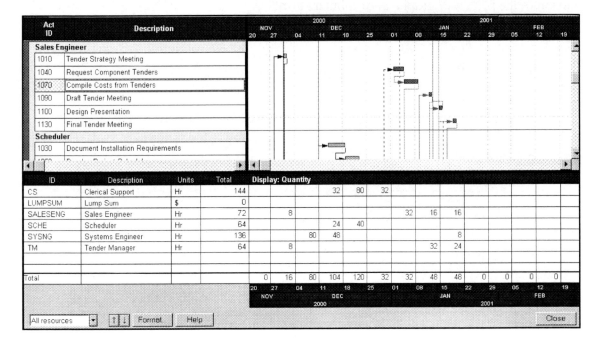

- **Format** is used in the same way as in the Resource Histogram.

- Select **View**, **Resource Legend** to display the **Resource Legend** on the screen.

18.6.3 Printing Resource Profiles and Tables

The printing options for Profiles and Tables are displayed by selecting **File**, **Page Setup**, **Resource Printing Options**:

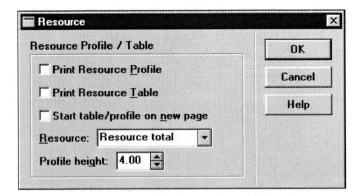

- You will have to reselect the resources you wish to display and print in the **Resources** box.

- The **Profile height** is used to prevent distortion of the output.

19 TOOLS AND TECHNIQUES FOR SCHEDULING

The following menu items are provided under **Edit**:

- Copy Picture
- Delete Activity
- Dissolve Activity
- Copy and Paste Cell
- Find Activity
- Select All
- Select Spotlighted
- Invert Selection
- Insert Recurring Activities
- Copy and Paste to and from Spread Sheets

19.1 Copy Picture

This allows a section or total screen to be copied to the clipboard. This may not be used for copying forms.

19.2 Delete Activity

This deletes the activity from the schedule. It deletes the relationships and activities in a chain have their chain broken.

19.3 Dissolve Activity

This deletes the activity from the schedule but preserves the logic by linking all **Predecessors** to all **Successors** with a Finish to Start relationship.

19.4 Copy and Paste Cell

You may copy information from one cell and paste into one or more cells by:

- Highlighting the cell you wish to copy
- Select Edit, Copy Cell
- Selecting one or more cells by dragging or using **Ctl** and click to select cells that are not adjacent to each other and
- Selecting Edit Paste Cell

19.5 Find

This option allows you to find any activity with data matching your defined criteria.

Select a data item from the **Find in:** drop-down list.

- Activity ID
- Any Activity Code
- Any Activity ID Code
- A Log Record
- Description
- Resource
- WBS
- Or All – to find data in all of the fields listed above

Select a value from the drop-down list that is not case sensitive. An asterisk "*" may be used as a wild card.

A date may be selected from the date drop-down box.

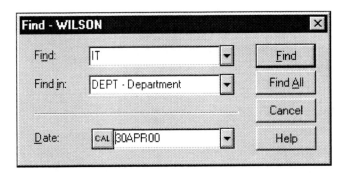

- **Find Next** finds the next occurrence.
- **Find All** selects all the activities that match the criteria.

19.6 Hide Activities

Select the activities or bands you wish to hide and then select **View**, **Hide.** Reapply a filter to display these activities.

19.7 Hide Topic Activities

View, **Hide Topic Activities** allows you to hide or display Topic Activities. This is a short cut to the option in you current layout found under **Organize**.

19.8 Select All

Select **Edit**, **Select All** or **Ctrl A**. This highlights and, therefore, selects all activities for operations such as Copy, Cut or emailing.

19.9 Select Spotlighted

Select **Edit**, **Select Spotlighted**. This highlights and, therefore, selects all activities that have previously been Spotlighted for an operation, such as copy, cut or for emailing.

19.10 Invert Selection

This selects all unselected activities and unselects all select activities.

19.11 Insert Recurring Activities

This allows the insertion of more than one activity that occurs on a regular basis. Select **Insert**, **Recurring Activity** to display the **Insert Recurring Activities** form.

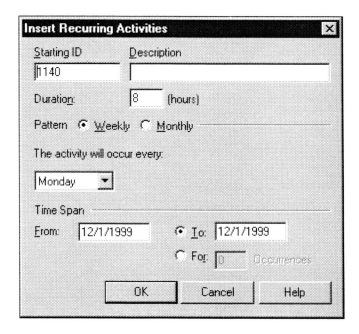

19.12 Copy or Cut and Paste to and From Spread Sheets

SureTrak will allow **Copy** or **Cut** and **Paste** to and from spread sheets, P3 and other packages. This may be useful for a number of purposes:

- Importing Activities from other applications

- Assigning Codes and Resources to Activities

- Statusing a schedule

- Saving Intermediate Baseline Dates

- Exporting Data to other packages

Copy or **Cut** copies the activity data from the columns in the schedule to the Windows clipboard.

- Move to the spread sheet application and paste. The activity information, including column header, is pasted into the application.

- Data may be edited or added.

- The activities may be selected and pasted back into the schedule with the normal SureTrak Paste Options.

To update resource data from a spreadsheet then:

- The schedule must be organized by resource

- The resource column must be available

19.13 Zoom, Zoom In and Zoom Out

Zoom, **Zoom In** and **Zoom Out** are used to increase or decrease the size of the display.

20 PROJECT UTILITIES

Under **Tools, Project Utilities** the following options are available:

- Back Up
- Restore
- Delete
- Check-in/Check-out

20.1 Back-up

Projects may be backed up to floppy disks or to other sub-directories on the PC or Network. It also allows file compression resulting in a single file per project with a PRX file extension.

Projects may be backed up with or without your layouts. If you wish to send your files to someone else it is best to include your layouts for them to use.

Remove Access List removes security restrictions from a P3 file so that it may be opened by anyone.

20.2 Restore

This restores backed up files.

20.3 Delete – Project

This deletes a project and ensures all files are deleted.

20.4 Check-in/Check-out

This is an option used when project groups are being utilized for multiple projects and is not covered in this manual.

21 WHAT IS NEW IN SURETRAK VERSION 3.0

The following is a list of the new features available in SureTrak Version 3.0.

- Long File Names

- Layout Tool Bar with Drop-Down Filters and Layouts

- Interactive Filters

- Modify Selected Bar

- Zoomed Timescale

- Timescaled PERT

- Web Publishing Wizard

- Resource Profile/Table Enhancements

- Primavera Post Office

21.1 Long File Names

SureTrak Version 3.0 is a 32 bit software and the standard format for SureTrak files now allows long file names (SureTrak Version 2.0 allowed a maximum of eight characters in the file name).

If you are using Concentric (P3) or Program Groups you are still restricted to a file name of 4 characters.

21.2 Layout Tool Bar with Drop-Down Filters and Layouts

A third tool bar has been introduced, the **Layout** toolbar, allowing faster access to layouts and filters. This toolbar is displayed and hidden by selecting **View**, **Layout Toolbar**.

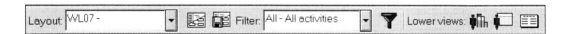

- Layouts and filters are selected using the drop-down boxes.

- The display in lower views may also be selected using this toolbar.

21.3 Interactive Filters

When you create a filter and tick the **Ask Me** box.

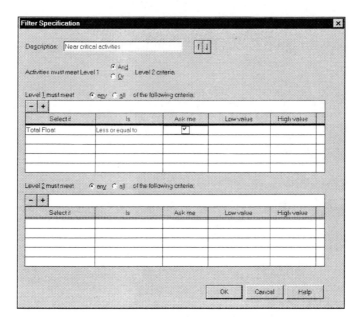

When you apply the filter you will be presented with the **Filter Value** form allowing you to nominate the value required for the filter.

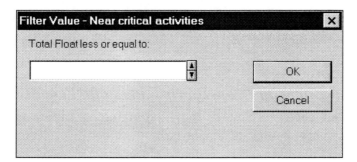

This feature is very useful as you now only need to create one filter which may be used for a number of purposes.

21.4 Modify Selected Bar

This new function allows you to modify one or more selected bars with color and style formatting.

Select one or more bars that require special formatting.

Then to open the **Modify Bar Elements** form select:

- Format, Bars, Modify Selected Bar… or

- Format, Selected Bars, Modify

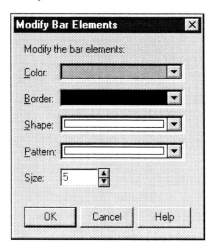

- **Color**, **Border**, **Shape and Pattern** are used to format the bars and points.

- **Size** determines the height of the bar or point.

The formatting may be copied and pasted to other bars and changed back to the standard format using the commands under **Format, Selected Bars**.

21.5 Zoomed Timescale

You may create a **Zoomed Timescale** area**,** which allow you to display a section of the bar area to have a different scale.

The example below has a Zoomed timescale from 1Jan00 to 21Jan00 with a daily timescale while the remainder of the schedule is weekly.

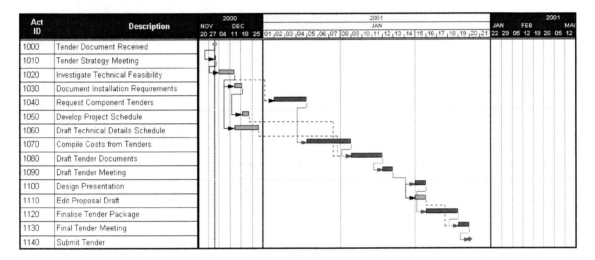

Select **Format**, **Timescale**, **Create a zoomed timescale area** to open the **Zoomed Timescale** form which allows the timescale to be zoomed into a smaller area than the entire project timescale.

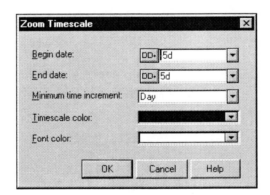

21.6 Timescaled PERT

SureTrak Version 3.0 has the facility for displaying a Timescaled PERT diagram which places the activities on a timescale. This option is found under **Format**, **Organize**, **Arrangement**.

Non Timescaled PERT Diagram

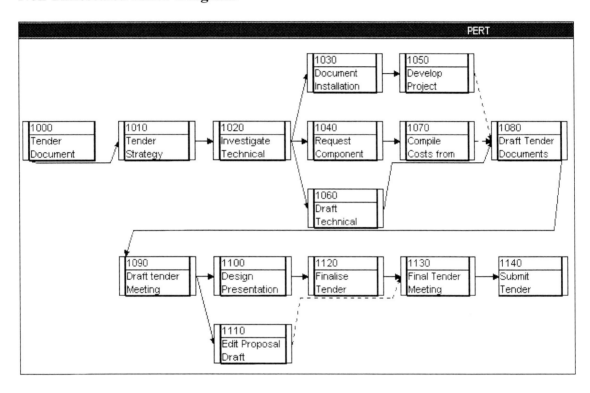

Timescaled PERT Diagram

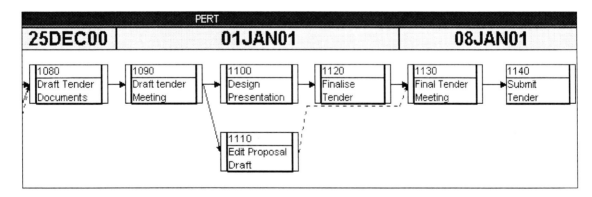

21.7 Web Publishing Wizard

This function allows you to save and publish reports on the web.

21.8 Save As Web Page

This function allows you to save a layout including the bar chart in graphical HTML format.

21.9 Resource Profile/Table Enhancements

The Resource Profile has a function to limit the value of the Y axis.

The Resource Tables now have row and column totals.

The Resource Profile and Resource Table may be accessed from the new **Layout Toolbar**.

21.10 Primavera Post Office

You are now able to collect and expected finish constraint using Primavera Post Office.

22 ITEMS NOT COVERED IN THIS BOOK

The following subjects are not covered in this book.

- Start Up Screen
- Summary Bars
- Statusing Project Data Using email using File, Mail
- World Wide Web Report Publishing
- SureTrak Mail
- Insert Object/Picture
- Insert Text/Hyperlink
- Insert Curtain
- Tools, Wizards
- Tools, Update Data Dictionary
- Tools, Basic Scripts
- Tools, Custom Tools, Modify Tools Menu
- Tools, Custom Tools, Excel Spell Check
- Tools, Custom Tools, Global Change and
- Tools, Custom Tools, Print Dictionaries.

Details of all these topics may be found in the User Manual and Help.

BOOKS PUBLISHED BY EASTWOOD HARRIS

ISBN: 0-646379-2-5-9

Project Planning Using Primavera SureTrak for Windows Version 2.0

Published 6 September 1999

ISBN: 0-957778-3-0-9

Planning Using Primavera Project Planner P3 Version 2.0

Published 16 March 2000

ISBN: 0-957778-3-1-7

Planning Using Primavera Project Planner P3 Version 3.0

Published 16 March 2000

ISBN: 0-957778-3-2-5

Planning Using SureTrak Project Manager Version 3.0

Published 27 June 2000

ISBN 0-957778-3-3-3

Planning Using Microsoft Project 2000

Published July 2002

ISBN 0-957778-3-4-1

Planning Using Microsoft Project 2002 Standard

To be published late 2002

Published by:
Eastwood Harris Pty Ltd
PO Box 4032
Doncaster Heights 3109
Australia

Distributed by:
Writersandpoets USA
2901 W. Queen Lane C
Philadelphia, PA 19129
United States

23 INDEX